DICKENS'S

GREAT EXPECTATIONS

D0088576

Other Books in the Christian Guides
to the Classics Series:

Bunyan's "The Pilgrim's Progress"

Hawthorne's "The Scarlet Letter"

Homer's "The Odyssey"

Milton's "Paradise Lost"

Shakespeare's "Macbeth"

DICKENS'S
GREAT EXPECTATIONS

LELAND RYKEN

CROSSWAY
WHEATON, ILLINOIS

Dickens's "Great Expectations"

Copyright © 2014 by Leland Ryken

Published by Crossway
    1300 Crescent Street
    Wheaton, Illinois 60187

Cover design: Adam Greene

Cover illustration: Howell Golson

First printing 2014

Printed in the United States of America

Scripture quotations are from the ESV® Bible (*The Holy Bible, English Standard Version*®), copyright © 2001 by Crossway. 2011 Text Edition. Used by permission. All rights reserved.

Trade paperback ISBN: 978-1-4335-3459-1
ePub ISBN: 978-1-4335-3462-1
PDF ISBN: 978-1-4335-3460-7
Mobipocket ISBN: 978-1-4335-3461-4

Library of Congress Cataloging-in-Publication Data

Ryken, Leland.
   Dickens's Great expectations / Leland Ryken.
     pages cm. — (Chrstian guides to the classics)
   ISBN 978-1-4335-3459-1 (tp)
   1. Dickens, Charles, 1812–1870. Great expectations. 2. Dickens, Charles, 1812–1870—Religion. 3. Virtues in literature.
4. Literature and morals. I. Title.
PR4560.R95   2014
823'.8—dc23   2013036215

Crossway is a publishing ministry of Good News Publishers.

BP		24	23	22	21	20	19	18	17	16	15	14
15	14	13	12	11	10	9	8	7	6	5	4	3	2	1

Contents

The Nature and Function of Literature

We need to approach any piece of writing with the right expectations, based on the kind of writing that it is. The expectations that we should bring to any work of literature are the following.

The subject of literature. The subject of literature is human experience, rendered as concretely as possible. Literature should thus be contrasted to expository writing of the type we use to conduct the ordinary business of life. Literature does not aim to impart facts and information. It exists to make us share a series of experiences. Literature appeals to our image-making and image-perceiving capacity. A famous novelist said that his purpose was to make his readers *see*, by which he meant to see life.

The universality of literature. To take that one step further, the subject of literature is *universal* human experience—what is true for all people at all times in all places. This does not contradict the fact that literature is first of all filled with concrete particulars. The particulars of literature are a net whereby the author captures and expresses the universal. History and the daily news tell us what *happened*; literature tells us what *happens*. The task that this imposes on us is to recognize and name the familiar experiences that we vicariously live as we read a work of literature. The truth that literature imparts is truthfulness to life—knowledge in the form of seeing things accurately. As readers we not only look *at* the world of the text but *through* it to everyday life.

An interpretation of life. In addition to portraying human experiences, authors give us their interpretation of those experiences. There is a persuasive aspect to literature, as authors attempt to get us to share their views of life. These interpretations of life can be phrased as ideas or themes. An important part of assimilating imaginative literature is thus determining and evaluating an author's angle of vision and belief system.

The importance of literary form. A further aspect of literature arises from the fact that authors are artists. They write in distinctly literary genres such as narrative and poetry. Additionally, literary authors want us to share their love of technique and beauty, all the way from skill with words to an ability to structure a work carefully and artistically.

Summary. A work of imaginative literature aims to make us see life accurately, to get us to think about important ideas, and to enjoy an artistic performance.

Why the Classics Matter

This book belongs to a series of guides to the literary classics of Western literature. We live at a time when the concept of a literary classic is often misunderstood and when the classics themselves are often undervalued or even attacked. The very concept of a classic will rise in our estimation if we simply understand what it is.

What is a classic? To begin, the term *classic* implies the best in its class. The first hurdle that a classic needs to pass is excellence. Excellent according to whom? This brings us to a second part of our definition: classics have stood the test of time through the centuries. The human race itself determines what works rise to the status of classics. That needs to be qualified slightly: the classics are especially known and valued by people who have received a formal education, alerting us that the classics form an important part of the education that takes place within a culture.

This leads us to yet another aspect of classics: classics are known to us not only in themselves but also in terms of their interpretation and reinterpretation through the ages. We know a classic partly in terms of the attitudes and interpretations that have become attached to it through the centuries.

Why read the classics? The first good reason to read the classics is that they represent the best. The fact that they are difficult to read is a mark in their favor; within certain limits, of course, works of literature that demand a lot from us will always yield more than works that demand little of us. If we have a taste for what is excellent, we will automatically want some contact with classics. They offer more enjoyment, more understanding about human experience, and more richness of ideas and thought than lesser works (which we can also legitimately read). We finish reading or rereading a classic with a sense of having risen higher than we would otherwise have risen.

Additionally, to know the classics is to know the past, and with that knowledge comes a type of power and mastery. If we know the past, we are in some measure protected from the limitations that come when all we know is the contemporary. Finally, to know the classics is to be an educated person. Not to know them is, intellectually and culturally speaking, like walking around without an arm or leg.

Summary. Here are four definitions of a literary classic from literary experts; each one provides an angle on why the classics matter. (1) The best that has been thought and said (Matthew Arnold). (2) "A literary classic ranks with the best of its kind that have been produced" (*Harper Handbook to Literature*). (3) A classic "lays its images permanently on the mind [and] is entirely irreplaceable in the sense that no other book whatever comes anywhere near reminding you of it or being even a momentary substitute for it" (C. S. Lewis). (4) Classics are works to which "we return time and again in our minds, even if we do not reread them frequently, as touchstones by which we interpret the world around us" (Nina Baym).

How to Read a Story

Great Expectations, like the other classics discussed in this series, is a narrative or story. To read it with enjoyment and understanding, we need to know how stories work and why people write and read them.

Why do people tell and read stories? To tell a story is to (a) entertain and (b) make a statement. As for the entertainment value of stories, it is a fact that one of the most universal human impulses can be summed up in the four words *tell me a story*. The appeal of stories is universal, and all of us are incessant storytellers during the course of a typical day. As for *making a statement*, a novelist hit the nail on the head when he said that in order for storytellers to tell a story they must have some picture of the world and of what is right and wrong in that world.

The things that make up a story. All stories are comprised of three things that claim our attention—setting, character, and plot. A good story is a balance among these three. In one sense, storytellers tell us *about* these things, but in another sense, as fiction writer Flannery O'Connor put it, storytellers don't speak *about* plot, setting, and character but *with* them. *About what* does the storyteller tell us by means of these things? About life, human experience, and the ideas that the storyteller believes to be true.

World making as part of storytelling. To read a story is to enter a whole world of the imagination. Storytellers construct their narrative world carefully. World making is a central part of the storyteller's enterprise. On the one hand, this is part of what makes stories entertaining. We love to be transported from mundane reality to faraway places with strange-sounding names. But storytellers also intend their imagined worlds as accurate pictures of reality. In other words, it is an important part of the truth claims that they intend to make. Accordingly, we need to pay attention to the details of the world that a storyteller creates, viewing that world as a picture of what the author believes to exist.

The need to be discerning. The first demand that a story makes on us is surrender—surrender to the delights of being transported, of encountering experiences, characters, and settings, of considering the truth claims that an author makes by means of his or her story. But we must not be morally and intellectually passive in the face of what an author puts before us. We need to be true to our own convictions as we weigh the morality and truth claims of a story. A story's greatness does not guarantee that it tells the truth in every way.

GREAT EXPECTATIONS

BY

CHARLES DICKENS.

IN THREE VOLUMES.

VOL. I.

LONDON:

CHAPMAN AND HALL, 193, PICCADILLY.

MDCCCLXI.

Original title page

Great Expectations: The Book at a Glance

Author. Charles Dickens (1812–1870)

Nationality. English

Date of first publication. 1861, in three volumes; published serially in 1860 in a British magazine founded, owned, and edited by Dickens.

Approximate number of pages. 450 (half as long as his typical novels)

Available editions. Multiple (Ignatius, Penguin, Norton, Barnes and Noble)

Genres. Victorian novel; coming-of-age story (a story that traces the development of the protagonist from childhood to adulthood); love story; gothic literature; suspense story

Setting for the story. Victorian (mid-nineteenth century) England; under that, the novel shuttles back and forth between an unnamed small town (real-life Rochester) and London.

Main characters. Pip, the first-person narrator who is the center of action at every point in the story; Joe Gargery, Pip's stepfather (technically his guardian), as well as the village blacksmith; Miss Havisham, a reclusive spinster in the hometown of the novel, unable to move beyond having been jilted on her wedding day; Estella, raised by Miss Havisham, a flirt who is the love of Pip's life; Abel Magwitch, a fugitive convict (eventually captured) who is the anonymous benefactor of Pip during Pip's period of great expectations as a privileged gentleman in London. In a Victorian novel there are numerous additional characters that we get to know well.

Plot summary. The novel follows Pip from ages seven to thirty-four. The orphaned Pip is raised by his ill-tempered sister and her husband Joe Gargery in a vintage British small town modeled on real-life Rochester. At the very start of the novel, Pip provides food for an escaped convict named Abel Magwitch. The convict flees from England and becomes prosperous, using his wealth to become the anonymous benefactor of Pip, now aged eighteen. Pip moves to London and lives a life of leisure as a young gentleman, based on the generosity of the anonymous benefactor. Underlying this external plotline are two more profound actions: (1) Pip's quest to become "respectable" defined according to the success ethic (worldly success as the goal of life), and (2) Pip's longing to win the love of the coquette (flirt) Estella. Those two "great expectations" of Pip come tumbling down when the convict arrives in London and announces himself as the mysterious benefactor. Pip's whole life now becomes absorbed in an unsuccessful attempt to smuggle Magwitch out of England. In the last phase of the story, Pip assumes a life of modest usefulness as an employee of his friend Herbert Pocket, whose business Pip had helped to finance with the money from his benefactor.

Structure and unity. (1) Dickens himself divided the story into three phases: Pip's abused childhood in "Hometown;" Pip's life of "great expectations" in London; Pip's departure from London and rebuilding of his life anew after his great expectations have been taken from him. The chronology of the hero's life thus organizes and unifies the novel. (2) A more interpretive grid can be placed on the threefold pattern just noted: Pip's virtuous (but unhappy) youth in an unsophisticated small town; his sophisticated life in London, accompanied by moral decline in his character; a synthesis of the previous two phases, as Pip builds a life that combines the small-town values of Pip's childhood with the growth in sophistication and education acquired during the period of his great expectations. (3) As suggested by the book's title, everything revolves around Pip's great expectations: the thing that gave rise to them, their nature, the mystery about who is financing them, their effects on Pip, his loss of them, and his coping with their loss.

Cultural context. *Great Expectations* epitomizes what we mean by Victorianism (the era named after Queen Victoria), but Victorianism encompasses an immense range of things. To begin, Victorianism perpetuated the Romantic movement that had dominated England in the first half of the nineteenth century. Romanticism elevated nature and feeling to supremacy, regarded the city as evil, protested social injustice and championed the cause of the downtrodden, feared the effects of the industrial revolution, was nostalgic for a simpler past, and focused on individual consciousness. *Great Expectations* is Romantic in all those ways. Victorianism then added ingredients to the mix: it was overtly Christian in its morality and belief system; it was an era of transition from the rural to the urban; it embraced a vigorous work ethic and middle-class morality; it was enamored of success and material prosperity, and from that evolved the optimistic philosophy known as progress (a belief that things were getting better with every passing year).

Tips for reading. (1) Dickens is one of the preeminent storytellers of all time, so the story qualities of *Great Expectations* need to form the basis for all other aspects of the enjoyment that we find in this novel. (2) Dickens is a master creator of characters, so we can expect to become acquainted with a gallery of memorable characters. (3) No author has excelled Dickens in the evocation of setting and atmosphere. (4) The subject of literature is recognizable human experience, and *Great Expectations* is a never-failing fountain of it. (5) The style in which Dickens expresses his content, and especially his way with words, needs to be relished. (6) Humor is never far from the surface in this story.

The Author and His Faith

Charles Dickens was the most famous novelist of the Victorian era in England. Christianity was the dominant belief system of his day. *Great Expectations* is Dickens's last great novel. It was written a decade before his death and is his "signature work," summing up his genius.

A rags-to-riches life. Charles Dickens became a legend in his own time. His childhood, though, was impoverished. When at age twelve his father was imprisoned for debt, Dickens was set to work in a shoe blacking factory. Dickens's route of escape from this life of early suffering was his writing, first as an editor and journalist and eventually as a writer of fictional stories. In addition to his fame as a writer, Dickens had an active career as a traveling lecturer (including trips to the United States), actor, and reader of his own stories. He was the supreme *litterateur* of his age. He led an overstimulated life characterized by fame, marital failure, and overwork.

Religious faith. The religion of Dickens is a complex subject. To start with the external facts of the matter, Dickens was raised in the Church of England, but in his early thirties he embraced Unitarianism. Dickens was outspoken about his impatience with the doctrinal details of the Christian faith and the institutional church. But Dickens also had many visible ties with the Church of England. His ten children were baptized in the Anglican Church. For most of his life he attended the services of the Anglican Church. He prayed in the morning and evening with his children. Dickens's final will (1869, a year before his death) includes the statement, "I commit my soul to the mercy of God through our Lord and Saviour Jesus Christ."

If we had only Dickens's writing as our source of information about his religious stance, we would conclude that he was broadly Christian in his beliefs and values. He respected both the New Testament and Jesus. He wrote *The Life of Our Lord* for his children so they would have a familiarity with the life of Jesus. The book is devoid of some of the supernatural and doctrinal aspects of Jesus's life, but reverential of Jesus as an example to emulate. When Dickens's children left home, he gave each of them a New Testament.

These biographical snapshots are a good avenue toward assessing the Christian element in Dickens. Dickens's religion stops far short of embracing the fullness of the Christian message, but much of the Christian faith is present. Certainly the moral vision of Dickens's fiction (its system of virtues and vices) is Christian. Allusions and echoes from the Bible and the prayer book abound. There is little in Dickens's fiction that is incongruous with Christian values and morality. It does not express the heart of the gospel of forgiveness of sins through the atonement of Christ. All of this requires a balancing act in which readers should neither underestimate nor overestimate the Christian element in Dickens's novels.

Storytelling Technique in Dickens

Storytellers like Homer, Chaucer, and Dickens, wrote C. S. Lewis, speak at once to every reader's imagination. This is a way of saying that some aspects of storytelling are universal—appealing to unsophisticated and sophisticated readers alike. Here is a list of what everyone likes in a story and that *Great Expectations* possesses in abundance:

- heroes and villains/heroism and villainy
- romantic love
- suspense and mystery
- adventure, danger, rescue
- conflict and its eventual resolution
- poetic justice (virtue rewarded, vice punished)
- striking and memorable characters
- a happy ending
- vivid settings; atmosphere
- dramatic irony
- reunion scenes
- comedy or humor

If we ask what the sophisticated reader wants, in addition to these elements that everyone likes, the answers include the following (and *Great Expectations* gives us these, too): (1) superior technique and artistry; (2) a sense of reality—an awareness that we are being put in touch with universal human experience as we assimilate the good story material noted above; (3) intellectual and moral significance; (4) depth of characterization (not simply an abundance of plot or action); (5) brilliance of style and skill with words.

Writers whose stories speak at once to every reader's imagination are good at characterization. When we praise a storyteller for skill in character portrayal, we ordinarily have the following in view (and again *Great Expectations* makes the grade easily):

- creation of universal character types, with the result that we feel as though we have met the characters in real life
- balancing that, the ability to create unique, one-of-a-kind characters (which usually embody, however, universal principles)
- vividness in physical descriptions of characters
- characters who elicit a strong reader response (whether of sympathy or aversion)
- satiric portraits (embodying human vice or folly)
- humorous characters that make us laugh

CHAPTER 1

Terror in the Churchyard

Preliminary note about format. Dickens published *Great Expectations* with chapters that bear numbers only, without titles. The descriptive chapter titles in this guide have been added to help us identify and remember what makes each chapter distinctive.

Plot Summary

Seven-year-old Pip is lingering in a churchyard (British term for a cemetery adjacent to a church) on a late winter afternoon. His parents and five siblings lie buried before him. In this spooky setting, "a fearful man" leaps from behind a tombstone and grabs Pip. The fearful man turns out to be an escaped convict, and his cross-examining of Pip yields him the information that Pip lives in the home of the local blacksmith. The convict turns Pip upside down and threatens him with death if he does not appear the next morning with a file and food. Thus terrorized, Pip "ran home without stopping."

Commentary

The opening page and chapter of a novel are the crucial test that every successful novelist must pass. The storyteller needs to put something in front of readers to draw them into the story and arouse enough interest to make them want to keep reading. Dickens has obviously cast his lot with the evocation of terror as his "hook" into the story. Everything that happens in this famous opening chapter evokes terror.

A good preliminary exercise for every episode in a story is to analyze what there is about the story material or technique that arouses our interest. Novelist E. M. Forster gives classic expression to this principle: a story "can only have one merit: that of making the audience want to know what happens next." Dickens has an unfailing knack for making us want to know what happens next.

Dickens is a master realist, basing his material on close observation of real life. Paradoxically, though, he makes continuous use of fairy tale material.

The first terror is the setting: winter, late afternoon, a churchyard, biting weather, an escaped convict capturing a helpless seven-year-old, a hangman's gibbet silhouetted against the sky. The process of interrogation that the convict imposes on Pip intensifies the terror. So do the threats that the convict unleashes, such as the threat to tear out Pip's heart and liver. The physical posture of Pip heightens the effect, as we see Pip shivering while sitting on a tombstone, being turned upside down so the bread in his pocket will fall out, and running home as the cattle lift their heads to stare at him.

But of course this is also our introduction to the first-person narrator and protagonist of the story. He is the archetypal child, first of all, and his way of thinking is naïve and childish. Second, he is an orphan, in important ways alone in the world, looking down at the graves of seven family members on the first page of the novel. Additionally, we catch an early glimpse of Pip's current family situation, with his sister as a sinister mother figure and the local blacksmith as a substitute father.

This chapter uses conventions of the opening of ghost stories: a figure of terror springs from behind a grave at twilight on a winter afternoon as the wind howls and a hangman's gibbet is silhouetted against the sky.

This novel is thoroughly rooted in the England of Dickens's day—so much so that it ranks as regional writing (writing that contains numerous references to a specific geographic region). One can go to a cemetery in Cooling in Kent and find the row of family graves that Dickens claims as the model for his description on the first page of this novel.

For Reflection or Discussion

Chapter 1 can be summarized under the formula "design for terror"; what things make up the terror? What feelings are evoked? What details show Dickens's skill at creating atmosphere?

An important feature of every story, but of a novel especially, is that the storyteller creates a whole world of the imagination that we enter as we read. The opening pages of a novel constitute our entry into that world. We need to operate on the premise that everything that the author includes is an important part of the world that gets set in motion as the story unfolds. Accordingly, noting the features of the imagined world is an important part of our analytic task.	**CHAPTER 2** # Terror at Home **Plot Summary** This chapter narrates what happened at home on the evening after Pip had been terrorized in the churchyard. Terror in the churchyard at the hands of a convict is now succeeded by a scene of abuse at the hands of Pip's sister, who functions in Pip's life as a surrogate mother. Most of the chapter is devoted to filling out the picture of Pip's home situation, through a pattern known as a foil (based on "to set off"). The unpleasantness of Pip's sister and the compassionate nature of Joe Gargery (who married Pip's sister and fills the role of father to him) stand out, highlighted by being contrasted to each other.

The second half of the chapter shifts from an emphasis on characterization (of Joe and his wife) to plot. We learn that the time is Christmas Eve and additionally that there has been an escape from the convict ship that is regularly docked in the marshes on the edge of town. This, of course, ties into the man who captured Pip in the churchyard and to whom Pip feels obliged to provide a file and food the next morning. Pip endures a sleepless night, ridden with anxiety about his morning mission. The chapter ends with Pip leaving the house and running "for the misty marshes."

Commentary

The first phase of a well-made plot is exposition—the dispensing of background information that readers need to know before the plot conflict can begin. In *Great Expectations* this exposition lasts for seven chapters. This chapter gives us a "slice of life" in Pip's home situation. It is a mixed situation, with the harshness of Pip's sister contrasted to the innate good nature of Joe Gargery.

Humor is a Dickens hallmark, and we need to be alert to it. Even in the most oppressive of situations portrayed in this novel, there is often a note of humor. For example, Pip sits in terror at the supper table because he needs to save bread for the convict, yet the whole scene in which he "bolts his food" is handled in a comic manner. Often it is Dickens's way of expressing something (his "way with words") that produces the humor, as when Pip describes his sister's practice of shoving him in irritation with the statement: "I often served as a connubial missile."

As the scene continues to unfold, Dickens skillfully introduces a note of foreshadowing about the action that we know will take place in the churchyard the next morning. The criminal motif will be of central importance in the story, and we are given a lot of information about an unusual feature of Pip's hometown, namely, the continuous presence of convict ships in the marshes, where criminals are set to work. The chapter ends on a note of high suspense as Pip steals a file and food and heads out for the marshes.

For Reflection or Discussion

What are the important features of Pip's home situation? Why do you think Dickens gave such a detailed picture of the domestic life in the Gargery household? What additional features of the world of the novel emerge in the chapter?

In the early chapters of *Great Expectations*, Dickens shows his genius at portraying childhood psychology. Much of it is humorous, as when on page one Pip concludes on the basis of the lettering on his parents' tombstones that his father was a "square, stout, dark man, with curly black hair," and his mother "freckled and sickly." But on a more somber note, we relive childhood fears as Dickens takes us inside the mind of the seven-year-old Pip.

One way in which storytellers make us want to keep reading is to create characters about whose destinies we are made to care. This applies preeminently to the protagonist and explains the leisurely pace of the novel in this chapter: Dickens wants us to get to know his protagonist and is in no hurry to return Pip to the marshes.

CHAPTER 3

In the Churchyard Again

Plot Summary

The design for terror continues in this episode. The scene is as spooky as it had been in chapter 1. A thick mist blankets the scene. The cattle stare in a frightening manner. We expect the worst. But at least we think we know what will happen, until Dickens springs a new terror on us: the first person Pip meets is, indeed, a convict, but not the one Pip had met the afternoon before. But Pip presses on with his mission and eventually comes to the original convict, who devours the food as a dog eats. Our curiosity is aroused (but not satisfied) when the convict is greatly agitated by the news of another convict loose in the region. The chapter ends on a note of high drama (a forte of Dickens) with the convict "filing at his iron [chain] like a madman."

In his classic short essay entitled "On Stories," C. S. Lewis makes it clear that he greatly values the quality of atmosphere in a story. Dickens is a master at creating atmosphere. Another way of getting at this quality of good stories is to say that world making is one of the most important tasks of a storyteller.

Commentary

The first thing to do is relish the descriptive genius of Dickens. No one has ever excelled Dickens's ability to describe the physical details of a setting. We also need to understand that this novel is "vintage British" in the pictures of landscape and weather that Dickens gives us. The means by which a storyteller awakens and maintains our interest are many, and one method is the creation of scenes that are so impelling to our imagination that we want to keep reading.

Balancing this attention to setting is the characterization of the original convict—the "fearful man," as he is called in chapter 1. We learn more and more about this figure—about his physical suffering on the cold marsh, his fear about being recaptured, and about his antagonism (not yet explained) toward the other escaped convict (an antagonism we only slightly detect, but that will explode just a few chapters later). A key moment occurs halfway through the chapter that would be easy to overlook entirely but that is actually one of the main events in the chapter. "Something clicked" in the throat of the convict, and Pip responds by feeling and expressing pity for the convict. Pip says, "I am glad you enjoy" the food. A bond has been established between Pip and the convict that will be a mainspring of the story's action.

For Reflection or Discussion

What descriptive touches are particularly striking? How does the convict come alive in your imagination as the chapter unfolds? At what moments do you sense that something has just happened that possesses a hidden and as yet unknown significance?

Great stories require that we reread them. On a first reading we are not fully aware of the eventual significance of certain details. This chapter is a prime example. It contains hints of things—clues laid down—that explode with significance when we reach later phases of the story. Two examples are the clicking in the convict's throat accompanied by Pip's gesture of compassion and the convict's intense and implicitly hostile feeling toward the other fugitive on the marsh.

CHAPTER 4

A Memorable Christmas Dinner

Plot Summary

Stories are constructed on the principle of a back-and-forth rhythm between contrasting elements. The first six chapters of *Great Expectations* keep alternating between the sinister marsh and the

Gargery house. Despite the obvious contrasts represented by this alternation, there are also things that remain constant across the chapters. The primary "constant" in these chapters is that adults terrorized the boy Pip.

The main action in this chapter is the account of Christmas dinner at the Gargery household. Four unforgettable local townspeople join the Gargery household for Christmas dinner. There is a double focus: the annual Christmas dinner rituals of a typical British household are reenacted before us, and we overhear the table conversation of this particular Christmas dinner. The element of terror stems from the fact that Pip knows all through the meal that in fulfilling his obligations to the convict he has (a) replaced the container of brandy with a bad-tasting mixture known at the time as Tar-water and (b) removed a much-anticipated pork pie from the pantry. The suspense becomes so unbearable for Pip that at the end of the chapter he makes a bolt from the table.

Commentary

Two things hold the key to the enjoyment of this chapter. First, it is a comic masterpiece. Highlights include the physical description of Uncle Pumblechook, the idiosyncrasies of personality among the guests, the conversation around the table, the style with which Dickens expresses certain things, and the scene in which Uncle Pumblechook drinks the horrible-tasting Tar-water.

Second, Dickens is often said to be "the man who invented Christmas" in England. This is of course an exaggeration, but the fact remains that in his Christmas stories Dickens codified the spirit and practices of English Christmas-

The comedy of this episode is unmistakable, but there is a dark underside as well: Pip continues to be mistreated by the adults. And this brings us to an important feature of the novel as a whole: convict and child are strangely bonded in this story, and what they have in common is that they are both outsiders in their society and at some level victims of it.

The British have always excelled in producing idiosyncrasies of character, and Dickens is a master at portraying them. The four new characters introduced into the story in this chapter are prime specimens, especially Uncle Pumblechook and Mr. Wopsle.

keeping. Chapter 4 of *Great Expectations* ranks as a "primary text" for documenting what Christmas was like in Victorian England. We need to allow Christmas dinner in the Gargery house to come alive in our imagination.

For Reflection or Discussion
What details constitute the humor of this chapter? What is the contrasting dark side of what happens around the dinner table? What makes a Victorian Christmas inviting as we reenact it in this chapter?

CHAPTER 5

Chase and Capture on the Marsh

Plot Summary
The Christmas dinner scene had ended with Pip bolting for the door, where he had run right into a soldier holding handcuffs. The party of soldiers has appeared on the Gargery doorstep in search of a blacksmith who can fix the handcuffs as part of their search to capture the escaped convicts. Quickly the action shifts to a chase scene on the marsh. Joe and Pip join the excitement of the chase. The convicts are captured, but the plotline does not exactly run in the conventional path. When the soldiers come upon the convicts, they are engaged in a life-and-death hand fight. One of the convicts is in extreme fear of the other, but at this point it is for us a mystery. The original convict sees Pip in the group, and in an effort to save Pip from reprisal in regard to the stolen food, he

The archetype at work in this chapter is familiar to storytelling and to real life. It is variously known as the "flight and pursuit" motif and the "chase and capture" motif. Literary critics would also identify the fight between the two convicts as a "scene of violence."

claims to have stolen it. Joe responds with sympathy to the convict, saying that he and Pip would not want a convict to have "starved to death, . . . poor miserable fellow-creatur." As in an earlier scene, something "clicked in the man's throat again." On a first reading, the detail seems unimportant, but it expresses the convict's emotional response to Pip and Joe's generosity and compassion. Later, the convict acts on his emotional reaction by becoming Pip's anonymous benefactor.

Commentary

Yet another genre to which this story belongs is the adventure story. Ernest Baker, in his book *A History of the English Novel*, has written, *"Great Expectations* is a novel of adventure, the sort of adventure that might well happen to a person who got himself mixed up with questionable characters, in such a spot as this, close to the convict-ships, or in what really were in those days the wilds of London."*

The back-and-forth swing of the story continues, but the first third of the chapter is a blend of the two story lines that have been emerging. The party of soldiers belongs to the convict story, but as Joe repairs the handcuffs, everyone else perpetuates the Christmas spirit as they stand around drinking wine and chatting. Then the warmth and confined space of the house is replaced by the "cold and threatening weather" and "the dismal wilderness" that the pursuers enter as they track the convicts. The relative quietness of the domestic sphere gives way to shouts and physical exertion. There is even a scene of violence as the two convicts fight each other. In the concluding sentence, the extinguishing of torches as they are "flung hissing into the water" brings this mini-adventure story to a close.

For Reflection or Discussion

What domestic touches serve as a balance to the dominant spirit of physical conflict and eventual violence of the action? If you are unfamiliar with the story as a whole, what details gesture toward some hidden significance? If you are familiar with the subsequent action, what significance do you attribute to such events as the accusations that the two convicts exchange and the conversation between the convict and Joe at the end of the chapter?

CHAPTER 6

Return to Normalcy

Plot Summary

In this brief chapter, Joe and Pip return home after the adventure of the convicts' capture on the marsh. The focus is on the loving relationship between Joe and Pip, with the hostility of Pip's sister toward him as a discordant counterthrust.

Commentary

This chapter serves the function of standing as a foil or contrast to the action narrated in the preceding five chapters. Virtually everything in the preceding six chapters has been extraordinary— once-in-a-lifetime events in Pip's life. This chapter represents a return to normal living. To enhance the sense of relief from violence, Dickens adds his usual humorous touches, as when Pip describes himself as "staggering on the kitchen floor like a little drunkard" when Joe finally removes him from his back, or the various theories about how the convict could have gotten into the pantry (which of course he never did) to steal the food.

For Reflection or Discussion

In what ways does this chapter give us a relief from the tension and chaos of the preceding five chapters?

Several archetypal character types are in full force in this chapter. Pip is the orphan boy, at the mercy of those who are willing to raise him. Pip's sister fills the fairy-story role of wicked stepmother in her mistreatment of her brother Pip and in her shrewish behavior toward her husband Joe. By contrast, Joe is the benevolent father figure who occasionally appears in literature.

CHAPTER 7
Pip's Childhood Education

Plot Summary

The general shape of *Great Expectations* traces the protagonist's life from childhood to adulthood. Education in school is a regular part of that development, so Dickens gives us a version of school in this chapter. The approach to the subject is satiric, as Dickens treats the education that Pip receives from Mr. Wopsle's great-aunt in a spirit of ridicule. But we do not dwell on the inadequacy of Pip's education for very long; instead Dickens shifts the focus to the relationship between Pip and Joe, starting with Pip's attempt to share some of his newly acquired learning with Joe.

As the conversation between Pip and Joe unfolds, Joe gives a glimpse of the dysfunctional family in which he was raised, with a father "given to drink." That, in turn, morphs into Joe's disclosure that when he married Pip's sister he had insisted that he would also provide for Pip. Pip melts with emotion, and when Joe also broaches the subject of his wife's shrewish behavior toward him and Pip, it proves such a landmark event that Pip could "date a new admiration of Joe from that night." All of this tenderness comes to an abrupt halt when Mrs. Joe arrives home and announces "in her snappish way" that a "Miss Havisham up town" wants Pip to come "to go and play there." Pip is duly cleaned up and put into a suit and sent to "play" at Miss Havisham's.

Much of the humor in Dickens's work consists of how Dickens expresses his content, and not necessarily because the situation itself is humorous. When Pip shows Joe a piece of his writing filled with misspellings, "Joe received it as a miracle of erudition." Mrs. Joe's ill-tempered behavior is expressed by Joe in terms of how "your sister is given to government." Pip's being scrubbed and dressed in a clean suit is described thus: "When my ablutions were completed, I was put into clean linen of the stiffest character, like a young penitent into sackcloth."

Commentary

At this point in the story we are still in the opening phase of the plot known as exposition. To devote fifty pages to exposition is an unusual strategy on the part of Dickens. We need to accept Dickens's game plan and understand that he wants to give us a full picture of life in "Hometown." The keynotes of this picture as it is extended into a seventh chapter are (a) the unsophisticated and intellectually impoverished situation in which Pip is raised (and from which he will become obsessed to escape), (b) the idealized character of Joe and of his nurturing behavior toward Pip, and (c) the emotional neediness of Pip (a wounded child if ever there was one).

For Reflection or Discussion

What elements of comic relief are present early in the chapter? How is Pip portrayed as emotionally needy? What things make up the idealized portrayal of Joe? How does Dickens's comic spirit show itself in this chapter?

CHAPTER 8

Pip's Initiation into Life at Miss Havisham's House

Plot Summary

This packed chapter is the longest chapter up to this point. The main action is Pip's first visit to Miss Havisham's house. In order to ensure his punctual arrival at the house of the mysterious Miss Havisham, Pip sleeps at the house of Uncle Pumblechook. When he stands before Miss Havisham's house at ten the next morning, he beholds a house "which was of old brick, and dismal, and had a great many iron bars to it." A sassy and in-

There are so many archetypes at work in this chapter that it is hard to imagine how such richness could converge in just one chapter. Miss Havisham is the reclusive spinster, as well as the spurned woman. Estella will eventually become the coquette or "tease," but at this early stage she is mainly the insulting girl. Pip is the child victim. Miss Havisham's house is the waste house—the deserted house with everything in disarray and decay. The adjacent garden is the deserted garden, with overtones of a lost garden of Eden.

The literary tradition of the gothic permeates the entire chapter. Gothic literature is a type of horror story, with the added element of the supernatural. Miss Havisham's house is a haunted house, with Estella as its guardian or gatekeeper and Miss Havisham as the resident ghost. The supernatural or phantom element appears at the end when Pip looks back at the house and incorrectly thinks that he sees "a figure hanging there by the neck."

sulting girl (later identified as Estella) ushers Pip into the room of Miss Havisham. It is a shocking place in every way, with everything in decay. It is in this chapter that we first learn the name of the house—Satis House (based on the Greek "enough"). There is no more famous literary house in British literature than Satis House.

Gradually a picture of Miss Havisham emerges. She is a psychotic, reclusive woman. The central fact of her life is that she was jilted on her wedding day. Ever since, she has worn white and in other ways wears clothing and jewelry suggestive of a wedding. She speaks to Pip of a broken heart and of needing diversion. That is where Pip factors in: he has been summoned to "play" for Miss Havisham. On this occasion the play consists of playing cards with Estella, who insults Pip as being "a common laboring-boy." Pip is ashamed of his common social standing and at the same time captivated by Estella.

After the card playing, Pip is led into a deserted garden adjacent to an abandoned brewery. Estella brings him food and drink. Pip feels so humiliated that he kicks the garden wall. He also recoils from the injustice of his mistreatment from Estella. Eventually Estella pushes Pip contemptuously through the locked gate at the front of the house. The final note is Pip's overwhelming sense of being "a common laboring-boy" with coarse hands and thick boots.

Commentary

We do not fully grasp on a first reading that the visit to Miss Havisham's house is the inciting moment in the well-made plot of this story. Given the general context of Pip's life as it was built up in our imagination for the first seven chapters, something is infused into the mix to get the plot conflicts started. Pip himself will "flag" the event in this way at the end of the following chapter: "That was a memorable day to me, for it made great changes in me." The change to which Pip refers is the awakening desire within him to rise socially beyond his current life in the blacksmith's house.

But that quest is still to come. In this chapter we are dazzled by the strangeness of everything (and by Dickens's inventiveness in composing that strangeness). Four things stand out. First is the spookiness of the place. The second is the characterization of the psychotic Miss Havisham and the disclosure of some of her pathologies (seriously aberrant patterns of behavior). Third, Estella is also introduced into the cast of "lead players" in the novel. On a first reading, we do not fully realize this, unless we know the conventions of the love story. If we have read enough love stories, Estella's insulting behavior toward Pip is a sure sign that the action will turn into a love story.

Finally, Pip's characterization receives major new development in this chapter. Pip's responses to what is inflicted on him by others (including Uncle Pumblechook in Pip's "overnight" and breakfast in his house) form the background chorus to the strange events happening in the foreground. The big change that engulfs Pip is that his discontent is aroused. The rising action phase of plot that will now unfold is the story of Pip's quest to rise socially, partly to become worthy of winning the love of Estella.

For Reflection or Discussion
The avenues toward exploring this chapter are numerous. One is to explore Dickens's inventive

All of the early stages of this novel contain hints of something that will eventually become a major part of the story but that on a first reading we overlook. When Estella resists the thought of playing cards with such "a common laboring-boy," Miss Havisham says under her breath, "You can break his heart." As the story unfolds, it turns out that this is exactly Miss Havisham's intention: she is the guardian of the orphaned Estella, through whom she sees a way to get revenge on males in the wake of her having been jilted on her wedding day.

imagination in producing such a bewildering array of strange and surrealistic places, people, and events. Additional questions to explore are the following: How does the chapter generate more sympathy for Pip as a victim? What universal experiences in real life are embodied in the figures of Miss Havisham and Estella? How does the chapter show affinities with the genre of the horror story?

CHAPTER 9
Debriefing Back Home

After the humor early in the chapter and the tenderness in the scene of Pip's confession to Joe, the last two paragraphs take us inside the consciousness of Pip. These paragraphs are crucial for understanding how Dickens wishes us to view the development of his protagonist and hero. As we listen to Pip's inner monologue, we share (1) his shame over his low social standing, (2) his exaggerated sense of the glamor of life for Estella and Miss Havisham, and (3) his self-awareness that the visit to Miss Havisham's house has completely revolutionized his aspirations in life.

Plot Summary

Pip returns home, where he is drilled with questions from his sister and Uncle Pumblechook about what took place at Miss Havisham's house. For undisclosed reasons, Pip does not rehearse what actually happened but instead fabricates a fictional and sensational story that borders on the fantastic. After Mrs. Joe and Uncle Pumblechook have had their curiosity satisfied, Pip finds himself alone with Joe and feels that he has betrayed Joe when he admits that the fabricated account was a collection of lies.

Commentary

The most obvious way to relish this chapter is to accept Pip's fabricated story of what happened at Miss Havisham's house as a comic tour de force. Having enjoyed the humor and relished Dickens's inventiveness in creating the details of Pip's story, we can discern serious issues at play. The fact that Pip's wild story is instantly believed shows the intellectual impoverishment of the society in which

Pip lives. We do not find it difficult to sympathize with the desire of a talented boy like Pip to achieve something better. Secondly, when Pip confesses his lies to Joe and feels that he has betrayed Joe, we see anew the mutual loyalty that exists between Joe and Pip.

For Reflection or Discussion

What details make this chapter a small classic of humor? What serious dimensions of Pip's characterization are developed?

CHAPTER 10

The Mysterious Stranger

Plot Summary

Since Pip's quest to rise socially has begun, he resolves to undertake the local version of formal education. He therefore decides to befriend a young girl named Biddy and learn from her "everything she knew." Biddy works at the school run by Mr. Wopsle's great-aunt, and we get a brief and satiric picture of an "Educational scheme or Course" that was a recognizable feature of Victorian life.

The main action in the chapter occurs at a local pub frequented by Joe. Its name is the Three Jolly Bargemen. One evening as Joe and Pip are seated in the pub a stranger sits at their table, orders a round of rum, pays particular attention to Pip, and stirs his own glass with the file that Pip had given to the convict in the churchyard. Then he gives Pip "a handful of small change." Pip is naturally conscience-smitten about this reminder of his association with convicts.

Dickens is a satirist par excellence. It is so natural to him that he is capable of including satire for its entertainment value, even when it does not play a major role in the overall story. If an exaggerated picture of a local school that doesn't quite make the grade is good for a laugh, Dickens is inclined to include it. Of course it is Pip's ambition to rise socially that enables Dickens to put the passage "on the agenda."

One of the ingredients that the popular imagination loves in a story is mystery. Dickens abundantly satisfies that taste in *Great Expectations*. While the mystery surrounding the stranger who stirs his rum with the stolen file is in itself a minor element in the story, it is the first tangible link between the convict and Pip after the opening events in the novel. In view of the major importance that the relationship between Pip and the convict has in the story as a whole, the evening in the pub emerges as a major instance of foreshadowing in the story.

Commentary

A literary critic has observed that all of Dickens's mature novels are at some level detective stories built around a central mystery and lesser ones as well. The episode that transpires on this evening at the Three Jolly Bargemen is one of these lesser mysteries. Who is the stranger who stirs his rum with the convict's stolen file and extends generosity to Pip? We are never told, though we can infer that he has been sent by the convict whom Pip helped at the beginning of the story. We end the chapter with a sense of "to be continued."

For Reflection or Discussion

The satiric account of the local "Educational scheme or Course" is a somewhat odd inclusion; what do you infer Dickens intended with this satiric account? Similarly, how does the mystery at the pub fit into larger designs in the novel? How does Pip's feeling of contamination (voiced at the end of the chapter) fit a pattern?

CHAPTER 11

Enter the Pocket Family

Plot Summary

When Pip arrives at Miss Havisham's house for his regular visit, it is Miss Havisham's birthday. Four relatives of Miss Havisham (including Sarah Pocket) are visiting her, flattering her in the hope of inheriting money from her. The conversation among these four and Miss Havisham is a dreamlike confusion, rendered even more bewildering by the sudden appearance of a burly man on the staircase who frowns at Pip and tells him to behave himself (we learn later that the man is the lawyer Mr. Jaggers).

Two further dimensions of the action are more obviously relevant to the ongoing action. First, the relationship between Estella and Pip is heading in the direction of a youthful romance. Estella is incorrigibly rude to Pip, but she also emerges as the archetypal coquette or flirt. She asks if Pip finds her "pretty." At the end of the chapter she invites Pip to kiss her on the cheek in a realistic version of a great archetype from ancient epic and romance literature—the distant lady's reward to an adoring knight after his victory in battle.

The part of the chapter that sparkles is the encounter between Pip and young Herbert Pocket. After playing cards with Estella, Pip is dismissed (as usual) to the deserted garden, where food is brought to him. This time he finds himself staring through a window at "a pale young gentleman with red eyelids and light hair." He is on the premises because of his relatives' visit for Miss Havisham's birthday. Foreshadowing his future characterization, Herbert has a greatly exaggerated sense of his ability. He challenges Pip to a fistfight and puts on a good show of knowing the rules of fighting, but is easily defeated by Pip.

Commentary

Comedy pervades the chapter. The flattering Camilla, hopeful of getting her hands on some of Miss Havisham's wealth, is scornfully ignored by Miss Havisham. Herbert Pocket's maneuvers while challenging Pip to a fight are hilarious, as is the irony of his complete inability to fight despite his knowing the rules and practicing all the right moves.

By this point in the story we have a general picture of Miss Havisham's house and surrounding area, but in this chapter we enter the surrealistic "inner sanctum" of a psychotic's residence. This being Miss Havisham's birthday, she visits a darkened room with a long table prepared for her wedding feast of long ago. All clocks have been stopped at the time Miss Havisham's wedding was set to begin. A wedding cake with spiders running in and out of it is on the table. Miss Havisham leans on Pip's arm while walking round and round the room. Miss Havisham's psychic state and abode are even more sinister than we had guessed.

Additionally, a now-familiar pattern in the early chapters of *Great Expectations* unfolds in this chapter: we are introduced to data that foreshadows later developments, but we do not realize this until the later events occur. Later in the story Herbert Pocket and Pip will share an apartment and become best friends and business associates. Here they are simply opponents in a fistfight.

For Reflection or Discussion

What new dimensions to the characterization of Miss Havisham emerge? What developments are hinted at in regard to the relationship between Estella and Pip? What comic moments do you relish? What gothic elements make the chapter come alive?

CHAPTER 12

Life at a Standstill

Plot Summary

The chapter opens with a nice piece of psychological realism: we are taken inside the youthful Pip's mind as he worries about being brought to justice for having beaten up Herbert Pocket. But his fears prove unwarranted, and his visits to Miss Havisham continue to run their boring course. Estella grows increasingly attractive, but the central part of the chapter is devoted to snapshots of Pip's unfulfilling life in the Gargery household. Finally, though, Miss Havisham follows through on the hints that Pip has been giving and announces that it is time for Pip to be apprenticed to Joe.

In the introduction to an older Penguin edition of *Great Expectations*, a literary critic named Angus Calder makes this helpful statement: Pip's life in his hometown "is one of minimal promise and thwarted potential." The novel implies "that once the ambitions (surely rightful) of an able boy like Pip have been awakened, such an environment is cramping and frustrating."

Commentary

The rising action has been running its course as we follow Pip's growing discontent with his status in life, accompanied by his quest to rise socially. The function of this chapter is one that is dear to story-tellers: Dickens builds up our sense of frustration that nothing is progressing for our sympathetic young hero, and then he springs a sudden break-through on us.

For Reflection or Discussion

What aspects emerge from this "slice of life" chapter that give us further insight into the situation from which Pip desires to be rescued? What new evidence is there that Miss Havisham has sinister designs against Pip in the person of Estella?

CHAPTER 13

Pip's Being Apprenticed to Joe

Plot Summary

While this is not the red letter day for which Pip might have hoped (escaping from "Hometown"), it is nonetheless a landmark day—the day of his being apprenticed to Joe. The momentous day begins with Mrs. Joe accompanying Joe and Pip to town. Joe is wearing his Sunday clothes. When the pair enters the room of Miss Havisham to receive her release of Pip from service, Joe is so ill at ease that he addresses Pip rather than Miss Havisham. Miss Havisham commends Pip's service to her and (amidst awkwardness) offers Joe twenty-five pounds as a reward for that service.

When Joe and Pip leave Miss Havisham and

join Mrs. Joe and Uncle Pumblechook, they proceed to the town hall for Pip to be officially sworn as an apprentice to Joe. Pip's sister insists on spending the twenty-five pounds at a celebratory meal at the Blue Boar Inn, and whenever Pip starts to fall asleep the adults wake him and tell him to enjoy himself. As often in this novel, the last paragraph takes us inside the consciousness of Pip, as we overhear his interpretive slant on what has happened.

The genre of the novel thrives on realism. Virtually every major detail of setting in the first third of *Great Expectations* is rooted in real-life Rochester. Even today one can walk the High Street of Pip's hometown. A visitor can stand in front of the model for Miss Havisham's house. The town hall where Pip's apprenticeship is sworn still stands on High Street, as does a façade of the former Victoria and Bull Hotel.

Commentary

The note of humor keeps breaking out, as it nearly always does in Dickens. The importance of the event to the progress of the plot is that it moves the young hero away from being under the authority of Miss Havisham. A new sphere of action opens up for both Pip and us as readers. The chapter thus serves as a transition, drawing closure to the Miss Havisham era and propelling us into life at the forge. Of course Miss Havisham will continue to intrude herself into Pip's life in ways that we cannot anticipate.

The concluding brief paragraph is what packs the real punch of the chapter. In it Pip shares with us his thoughts as he got into his "little bedroom" at the end of this momentous day. His verdict: "I was truly wretched, and had a strong conviction on me that I should never like Joe's trade."

For Reflection or Discussion

What touches of humor light up the chapter? In what ways is the chapter a bridge between phases of action?

CHAPTER 14

Ashamed of Home

Plot Summary

The brevity of this two-page chapter is an anomaly in *Great Expectations*. It is in effect a soliloquy in which Pip shares his extreme unhappiness about his home and its routines.

Commentary

The keynote of the chapter is sounded in its first sentence: "It is a most miserable thing to feel ashamed of home." After that, we get variations on the theme of Pip's discontent with his current life.

For Reflection or Discussion

This is a depressing chapter, but it expresses a side of life that everyone knows; with what features do you resonate? How do you come to terms with those feelings?

The point of view in *Great Expectations* is known as first-person narrative, meaning that the narrator speaks for himself and uses the pronouns *I, me,* and *my.* This strategy takes us right inside the thought process of the narrator and protagonist. Often in literature the first-person point of view takes a confessional turn, as the narrator confesses personal failing. Chapter 14 is a masterpiece of confessional writing.

CHAPTER 15

Violence at Home

Plot Summary

After the single focus of the preceding chapter devoted to Pip's discontent, this chapter explodes with multiplicity. It starts with a brief account of the conclusion of Pip's formal education (rudimentary as it was) and of his complete failure (despite good intentions) to pass on his knowledge to Joe. Pip proposes that he visit Miss Havisham (and we know why), and Joe assents. But before

Pip can make the visit, Dickens visits a scene of violence on us.

We are introduced to a villainous journeyman hired by Joe at the forge. He is named Orlick, and "he never even seemed to come to his work on purpose, but would slouch in as if by mere accident." In this part of the story, Orlick objects that Pip is given time off to go up town to visit Miss Havisham. Mrs. Joe overhears the conversation and makes a snide comment about Orlick's being a "great idle hulker." Orlick insults Mrs. Joe, Joe feels obliged to defend his wife's honor, and a fight ensues.

When Pip arrives at Miss Havisham's house, he faces a great disappointment: "No Estella." Miss Havisham's explanation: "Abroad, educating for a lady; far out of reach; prettier than ever." As Pip trudges homeward in the darkness and rain, he is unexpectedly joined by Orlick, who alerts him that convicts have again escaped from the prison ships. When the pair comes to the Three Jolly Bargemen, Pip is told to run home, as Mrs. Joe has been physically attacked while Joe was away from the house.

One of Dickens's greatest gifts as a writer is his descriptive ability. The fourth paragraph of this chapter is a classic; it starts with the statement, "It was pleasant and quiet, out there with the sails on the river. . . ." Occasionally *Great Expectations* falls into the genre of nature writing.

Commentary

This is a "catch all" chapter and "slice of life" chapter. The main new element is the addition of the villainous Orlick to the cast of characters. Orlick will be important from this point to the end of the book (though at first reading we have no way of knowing that). He is a one-of-a-kind character, especially in the detail that he never seems to come to work on purpose but to slouch in by mistake. Two Orlick-related events take most of the space in the chapter. One is the fistfight between Joe and Orlick, which we relive from start to finish, ending with "that singular calm and silence which succeed all uproars." Second, Orlick comes out of the darkness to join Pip on his walk back to the village. We could as well be watching a crime show, replete with bad people in unexpected places, perhaps trying to establish alibis.

The early part of the chapter, recounting a typical Sunday afternoon with Joe "greatly enjoying his pipe," functions as a foil to the sensational events noted above. The quietness of the opening paragraphs is also a contrast to the crime scene at the Gargery house in the last paragraph, where we read that "it was full of people; the whole village was there."

For Reflection or Discussion

This chapter continues to create a whole world of the imagination that we enter as we read; whereas in the middle of the book we will enter the world of London, in the first third we are thoroughly immersed in the world of small-town England. For you, what are its main features? What do you find attractive, and what do you find unattractive?

For all the depth of characterization and significance of content that we find in *Great Expectations*, the novel also has such an abundance of exciting and even sensational action that at the plot level it belongs to the genre known as melodrama. Melodrama is characterized by sensational settings and external action, polarized characters (characters either very good or very bad), and a simple moral scheme in which virtue and vice are obvious. *Great Expectations* is *more* than a melodrama, but as a work of the "popular" imagination it has elements of melodrama.

CHAPTER 16

Crime Scene

Plot Summary

The preceding chapter had ended with Pip's arrival at his house, astir with onlookers of a crime. This chapter fits right into the conventions of the crime documentary on television. We are gradually given the details of what has happened, as policemen and detectives (some of them from London, no less) ply their trade before us. The essential information is that Mrs. Gargery was viciously struck on the head and spine with a blunt instrument, and further that the instrument was "a convict's leg-iron which had been filed asunder." Part of the pathos of the situation is that Mrs. Gargery's "temper was greatly improved, and she was patient."

A second major event occupies the second half of the chapter, though on a first reading we have no way of knowing that it will loom so large. A local girl named Biddy (approximately the same age as Pip) becomes a permanent member of the Gargery household as a housemaid. Biddy has already figured as a helper at the local school where Pip attended. We do not lose sight of the crime, however. We learn that Pip's sister has a way of repeatedly drawing the letter T on a slate. Pip eventually concludes that the object represents a hammer, and when presented with the possibility Biddy at once identifies Orlick as the attacker. Pip's sister, instead of being hostile to Orlick, "manifested the greatest anxiety to be on good terms with him."

Commentary

If we have watched crime documentaries or detective stories on television, we know exactly what is happening in this chapter. Policemen and detectives are on a crime scene gathering evidence. As onlookers, we are gradually given bits and pieces of data. Within the general category of crime story, we have a specific subgenre that we can call "with a blunt instrument." In the text, we read that Mrs. Gargery "had been struck with something blunt and heavy, on the head and spine." Obviously Dickens creates a self-respecting physical attack.

In real life as in crime fiction, once the crime

Even though *Great Expectations* was originally composed and published as a serial (a series of monthly installments in a magazine), obviously Dickens had the entire concept worked out from the beginning. Among several key relationships that Pip has in the story, one of them is established in the opening chapter when Pip encounters the convict. From time to time Dickens reintroduces the convict into the story. In this chapter that takes the form of Pip's brooding over the importance of the fact that the convict's leg-iron was found at the scene of the crime.

scene has been assembled before us the story takes the direction of a "who-done-it" story. Often the clues are completely inexplicable, and Dickens complies with the convention. We are mystified by the fact that on the crime scene is "a convict's leg-iron which had been filed asunder." And then of course there is the process of speculation of who committed the crime. Although Mrs. Gargery was not murdered, in every other way this chapter fits the pattern of what we call a murder mystery.

For Reflection or Discussion

In what ways does Dickens show his mastery of the conventions of the "murder mystery?" In this genre, it is only natural that the readers or viewers reach their own conclusion as to who committed the crime; based on the clues, what is your own guess?

CHAPTER 17

Pip at the Crossroads: A Sunday Afternoon Walk with Biddy

Plot Summary

The main action is a Sunday afternoon walk and conversation involving Pip and Biddy. The subject of the conversation ranges over many topics, but the point of departure is Pip's disclosure to Biddy, "I want to be a gentleman." In this chapter, therefore, Dickens provides a full airing to the rising action phase of this well-made plot, namely, Pip's drive to rise socially beyond his present humble standing. Pip's discontent is thus one strand that we can trace in the Sunday afternoon conversation between Pip and Biddy. A summary statement comes in the second paragraph: "I continued at heart to hate my trade and to be ashamed of home."

Somewhat surprisingly, Biddy herself also becomes a continuous subject of the conversation. Early in the chapter we learn that Biddy has absolutely blossomed as housemaid in the Gargery household. We learn variously that "she was not beautiful—she was common," that she is "one of those who make the most of every chance," and that she "was the wisest of girls."

A third strand in the conversation is the interaction between Pip and Biddy. Pip's discontent (and his continuing infatuation with the exotic Estella) is challenged by the worthiness of Biddy and the life of the forge. Repeatedly Pip expresses such sentiments as "if I could only get myself to fall in love" with Biddy, or, "It was clear that Biddy was immeasurably better than Estella, and that the plain honest working life to which I was born had nothing in it to be ashamed."

At the end of the chapter we return to the who-done-it motif as Orlick meets Pip and Biddy in the churchyard. Biddy refuses his suggestion that he accompany the pair home, offering reasons to Pip for her dislike of Orlick.

Commentary

Dickens has an uncanny mastery of the pace of a story. After a flurry of exciting external action in the preceding scenes devoted to the crime at the Gargery house, this chapter is internal in its scope. The real subject is Pip's development as a character. More specifically, we are taken inside his inner dilemma and turmoil as he takes stock of his dis-

Much of *Great Expectations* belongs to the realm known as melodrama. But Dickens is equally a master at capturing the inner life of the mind and soul. In this chapter he takes us on a psychological and moral journey into issues of life that are very deep and universal.

content. The main action is internal, and in the very last paragraph Pip himself speaks of being "at the height of my perplexities." Pip is drawn in two directions: something inside him longs for the excitement of the exotic (being a gentleman, winning the love of Estella), and yet his reason tells him that the common life (including the homespun worthiness of Biddy) is morally better than the exotic life. Dickens has captured both the psychological and moral aspects of the dilemma with clarity.

In the next-to-last paragraph, Pip's musings fall upon a subject whose importance we could easily miss (something that is repeatedly true of this subtle novel). Pip speaks of his scattered thoughts being intermittently focused by a single thought—"that perhaps after all Miss Havisham was going to make my fortune when my time [as Joe's apprentice] was out." When Pip comes into his "great expectations" through the generosity of an anonymous benefactor, he will mistakenly think that Miss Havisham is his benefactor, and even that she is grooming Estella to be his beloved.

For Reflection or Discussion

What things make up the moral reasoning and vacillation of Pip as he wrestles with the conflict between his longing for the distant and mysterious (perhaps with a touch of the forbidden) and his knowledge that the common is worthy? What is universal in the dilemma that is posed in this chapter? How do you assess and respond to the characterization of both Biddy and Pip as the chapter unfolds? In what direction do you wish Pip to resolve his dilemma?

The characterization of Biddy in this chapter (and subsequently) is governed by an important archetype of literature and life. It is known as "the girl next door," or "the boy next door." Such a person is good, solid, dependable, and practical, but lacking the "otherness" that a person subconsciously searches for in a marriage partner. By contrast, Estella abundantly embodies that "otherness" and excitement, but the tragedy of Pip's infatuation with her until the very end of the novel is that she is unworthy of Pip's love.

CHAPTER 18

Pip's "White Knight" Arrives

Plot Summary

As noted earlier, the rising action phase of this plot is Pip's quest to rise socially. The single most important event in this quest occurs in this chapter with the arrival of a lawyer from London carrying an announcement that Pip has come into a large fortune. The lawyer is named Mr. Jaggers (another major addition to the cast of characters), a wealthy criminal lawyer.

Mystery surrounds Pip's new situation. Someone has come out of nowhere (it seems) to confer on Pip "a handsome property," meaning a lavish monthly income. A requirement is that Pip "be immediately removed from his present sphere of life" and be "brought up as a gentleman" or "young fellow of great expectations." This means moving to London. Further, the identity of the benefactor is to remain "a profound secret." Pip's imagination rejects the latter requirement, and he immediately concludes that "Miss Havisham was going to make my fortune on a grand scale." Once the lawyer asks, "When will you come to London?" the entire focus of action turns in the direction of Pip's leaving home.

Commentary

Pip's coming into his fortune is the key event in the rising action of this well-made plot, which can be formulated as "Pip's quest to rise socially." Once the excitement of the announcement settles down, we see Pip's changed relations with Joe and with Biddy. It is painful to watch. In a key statement

Dickens apparently had the master plan of his stories in his head at all times. On the occasion of Pip's second visit to Miss Havisham's house, when the relatives were visiting Miss Havisham on her birthday, an imposing man had spoken harshly to Pip. In the current chapter we find out this man was none other than Mr. Jaggers. We cannot help wondering what he was doing at Miss Havisham's house.

The last four paragraphs of the chapter are devoted to Pip's thoughts when he returns to his tiny bedroom at the end of this momentous day. Dickens's writing and insight into the interior life are at their best in these paragraphs.

from Pip, we read that "as Joe and Biddy became more at their cheerful ease again, I became quite gloomy. Dissatisfied with my fortune, of course, I could not be; but it is possible that I may have been, without quite knowing it, dissatisfied with myself."

For Reflection or Discussion

One of the ingredients of well-told stories is an element of surprise; what developments narrated in this chapter surprise you? As the momentous external events unfold, what story of interior action within the mind of Pip is also told?

CHAPTER 19

Pip Says Good-Bye to the Village

Plot Summary

This chapter narrates Pip's final days and hours in the village before embarking for London. The exterior action involves Pip's preparations for his move: reaching closure with acquaintances (especially Joe, Biddy, and Miss Havisham), getting fitted for new clothes, packing his boxes. The interior action is the running commentary that Pip shares with us regarding his responses to these external events. True to life, Pip's responses are a bundle of contradictions. On the one hand, he is glad to be able to say "farewell, monotonous acquaintances of my childhood, henceforth I was for London and greatness."

But nearly everything in this positive vein is undermined by sadness at leaving. Pip welcomes the thought of doing good for Joe now that he has the means to do so, but when he proposes that Biddy undertake an improvement of Joe's manners in preparation of Pip's doing something for him, Biddy is defensive on Joe's behalf, and the conversation ends in unpleasantness. It is exciting to be fitted for new clothes, but when Pip tries the new clothes on, they "were rather a disappointment, of course." The leave-takings and good-byes are also somber and heavy. Already Pip's great expectations fall a bit short.

But there is high comedy as well as pathos in the chapter. Uncle Pumblechook is a spectacle of good will toward Pip, now that he has risen in society. Sarah Pocket, successor to Estella as gatekeeper for Miss Havisham "positively reeled back when she saw" Pip in his new clothes. True to life, on the night before Pip's departure to London, he has wild dreams, including one of coaches going to wrong places in London and "having in the traces, now dogs, now cats, now pigs, now men—never horses."

The ending of the chapter is imposing, and the last sentence is an implied allusion to the last lines of *Paradise Lost*. In Milton's poem, as Adam and Eve leave Paradise, we read that "the world was all before them." Dickens echoes this with the sentence, "And the mists had all solemnly risen now, and the world lay spread before me." After the chapter itself Dickens inserts as a marker the sentence, "THIS IS THE END OF THE FIRST STAGE OF PIP'S EXPECTATIONS."

Dickens had such a way with words that he could make moments immortal. When has a breakfast roll ever had the following degree of immortality thrust upon it? "Mr. Trabb had sliced his hot roll into three feather beds, and was slipping butter in between the blankets, and covering it up." And then there is the true-to-life picture of Mr. Trabb's response when Pip announces that he has come into money: "Mr. Trabb forgot the butter in bed, got up from the bedside, and wiped his fingers on the table-cloth, exclaiming, 'Lord bless my soul!'"

Commentary

Dickens's game plan in this chapter is to juxtapose two contradictory experiences, and we can trace each one systematically through the chapter. One thread is positive and consists of Pip's eagerness to enter an exciting new phase of his life. He can't wait to get to London. The other thread is negative and consists of reluctance to leave the village and sadness to be saying farewell. The unifying element in this web of contradictions is that everything revolves around the motif of leaving home.

There is a wealth of universal human experience in this chapter. Everyone knows what it is like to anticipate a new phase of life. Pip's longings are our longings. Equally, most know the sadness that accompanies permanently leaving home and saying good-bye to friends and family members. Many readers have experienced the need to buy new clothes in preparation for a move to a new situation.

For Reflection or Discussion

What details and passages contribute to the positive theme of anticipation of something better? What passages fit into the opposite mood of sadness over leave-taking? Dickens has gotten inside the experience of ending a phase of life and departing for a new life; with what aspects of this chapter do you particularly resonate? What similar events in your own life are given form and shape in this chapter? How do you respond to Pip as he shares his inner thoughts and feelings?

Since Pip mistakenly assumes that Miss Havisham is his benefactor, special importance attaches to the words that he exchanges with her when he pays a good-bye visit to her. As we read the passage, various details make it easy for us to share Pip's assumption that Miss Havisham is the source of Pip's money.

CHAPTER 20

Arrival in London

Plot Summary

Pip makes the five-hour journey "from our town to the metropolis" of London. It is a brave new world for the boy from the small town. Pip goes to the address given him by the lawyer Mr. Jaggers (his new guardian), and it turns out to be the law offices of Mr. Jaggers. Pip is "fascinated by the dismal atmosphere of the place." Since Mr. Jaggers is occupied at court, Pip tells the clerk that he will take a walk in the neighborhood. The neighborhood is in the heart of the city of London, and the first sights of the city give Pip "a sickening idea of London."

When Mr. Jaggers arrives on the sidewalk, he interacts with a number of people who are standing about. It is a confusing series of exchanges about lawyers, clients, and potential witnesses. We are left with an unsettled feeling about such a feared figure as Jaggers, but there can be no doubt that he is successful at his profession. In a brusque statement, Jaggers tells Pip, "Of course you'll go wrong somehow, but that's no fault of mine," and then he sends Pip with his office clerk, John Wemmick, to the apartment that has been rented for him.

Commentary

Pip reenacts an important archetype in this chapter. It is the initiation motif—a character's experience of something for the first time. Pip is the boy from the small town being initiated into the big city. A good way to organize our experience of this chapter is to view ourselves as the observant trav-

This chapter is filled with specific place names—Little Britain [a street name], Cheapside, Bartholomew Close, Smithfield [full name in real life: Smithfield Market], St. Paul's [Cathedral], Newgate Prison. It is important to know that all of these are real places that can be visited today (or at least modern versions of the ones named in the novel). This novel remains one of the best introductions to the places and social tenor of England and the English people.

eling companion of Pip, experiencing the sights and sounds of the city of London. Like cities in real life, the London that we encounter in this chapter is a combination of the dazzling and the sordid, the exciting and the cheap-and-tawdry.

We are also initiated into the legal and judicial world of Jaggers and his office workers. There is something symbolic about Dickens's decision to make a law office the point of entry into London, inasmuch as it epitomizes the power and affluence that Pip hopes to attain. But Dickens's social protest also underlies the chapter. Dickens never forgave the judicial system for the injustices it inflicted on his family and others, and by the time this story ends, this note of social protest will become a major aspect of *Great Expectations*. Certainly in this chapter Dickens paints a heightened contrast between the power of the privileged class and the desperation of the lower class (as represented by the people who mill about Mr. Jaggers when he makes his way down the sidewalk).

"Of course you'll go wrong somehow," predicts Mr. Jaggers to Pip. There is an additional archetype at work here. It is the pattern of a young person from a rural and small-town background leaving that environment behind, going to the city, and being corrupted by it. Although Pip never becomes a fully depraved person during his period of great expectations, in a modified sense he undergoes a moral decline from his childhood in the village.

The archetype of the young person from the country ruined by the city was important in both England and America in the latter nineteenth century. It resulted in a genre of American literature known as the city novel. Obviously this genre summed up a fear of the big city, especially in its influence on people from a simple rural background.

For Reflection or Discussion

What stands out for you in these early glimpses of the London of this novel? What principles govern Dickens's selectivity of details? What does Dickens say about life and values by means of this picture of the city? What small signs are present from the beginning that Pip's "great expectations" will not be as great as anticipated? What assessment do you make of Mr. Jaggers?

CHAPTER 21

From Law Office to Pip's Apartment

Plot Summary

The preceding chapter represents Pip's arrival in the public world of London. This chapter moves him from Jaggers's law office to the apartment selected for Pip. The person who leads Pip through the streets of central London is John Wemmick, a clerk in Jaggers's office. Wemmick will become one of the most interesting and rounded characters in Pip's circle of acquaintances, but this chapter gives us only first impressions (as in real life).

The walk allows for Dickens to record snapshots of Victorian London, mingled with conversation between the experienced Wemmick and the initiate Pip. When the pair arrives at Barnard's Inn, the apartment building where Pip will reside, they are met by Pip's apartment mate Herbert Pocket.

Commentary

Several literary motifs converge in this ostensibly low-voltage chapter. As Pip walks from Jaggers's law office to his apartment, he continues to fill the role of the initiate—the inexperienced boy from the village encountering the sights of London for the first time. His inexperience sometimes pro-

Wemmick says to Pip, "*I* was new here once." Part of the humor of this chapter consists of the gap between the now-experienced city person Wemmick and the naïve boy from the country. As always with great literature, we look *through* the literary text to our own similar experiences of life. We all know what it means to be the inexperienced person dazzled by the superior knowledge of a person who "knows the ropes."

duces humor. Pip's responses to his first glimpses of London also hint that this place of great expectations will prove somewhat disappointing.

Additionally, Dickens shows such familiarity with the city of London that much of the remainder of the novel is a version of regional writing. Within that category literature that portrays a specific city in realistic detail constitutes a genre loosely called "the literature of the city," just as writing that describes nature is "nature writing." One avenue toward enjoying this chapter is to relish Dickens's skill at description.

For Reflection or Discussion

What touches of humor enliven the chapter? As you undergo Pip's experiences with him, what captures your attention as you (along with Pip) are initiated into the city of the novel? The power of fiction resides in the element of transport from our own time and place to another time and place; how does Dickens's skill with description and inventiveness of detail enable that transportation in this chapter?

Walking the streets of London (as Wemmick and Pip do in this chapter) is something that Dickens did throughout his life. The practice started in earnest when twelve-year-old Dickens walked the streets by night as a respite from his twelve-hour working days in the shoe blacking factory. In his years as a writer, he walked to gather materials for his imagination and as an aid to composition. But eventually he walked excessively and finally to the ruin of his health.

CHAPTER 22
Meet Herbert Pocket

Plot Summary

The plotline is simple: having arrived at his London apartment, Pip meets the person who is currently living there and who will occupy the apartment with Pip. We are as surprised as Pip to learn that the person is Herbert Pocket, the boy who a few years earlier had been such a pushover during the fight in Miss Havisham's garden. With greetings having been exchanged, the conversation naturally turns to Miss Havisham (cousin of Herbert's father). Along with Pip, we learn about Miss Havisham's wedding day trauma as the origin of her psychotic behavior. We also learn that Estella is the adopted daughter of Miss Havisham.

The second half of the chapter fills in the picture of Herbert and his family. Herbert has a minor job as a clerk in a firm that insures ships, but in his imagination he has grand dreams of making a fortune in trading and investment. Shortly after this first evening meal in the apartment, Pip is invited to visit the Pocket household in Hammersmith. As is true of many scenes in Dickens, it is a one-of-a-kind experience.

This chapter is one of Dickens's comic masterpieces. Much of it focuses on Herbert Pocket, the dreamer, and on his family. This suggests that a particular branch of Dickens's humor is domestic comedy, involving families and meals.

Commentary

One piece of narrative business in this chapter is to introduce us to Herbert Pocket as a full-fledged character. He is one of Dickens's most famous portraits. The key to his personality is that he is a "romantic" dreamer, out of touch with reality. The first index to this occurs when he apologizes to Pip for having "knocked [him] about so" during the fight in Miss Havisham's garden. More extravagantly yet, he talks at length about making a fortune someday when in fact he has a very undistinguished desk job in the office of an insurance company. As Pip correctly notes, "having already made his fortune in his own mind," he acted as though it were a fact accomplished.

A second important development in this chapter is the wealth of new information about Miss Havisham and her tangled web of relationships. There is more than we can fully grasp on a first reading, but the picture is getting clearer. Equally importantly, we will later be able to look back at these disclosures of Herbert as a foundation for understanding eventual developments.

And then there is the unforgettable Pocket family, where the children "were not growing up or being brought up, but were tumbling up." It is a comically dysfunctional family, partly rendered such by the aristocratic pretensions of Mrs. Pocket. Later in the novel we will learn that Mr. Pocket goes out lecturing on household management! This novel is filled with pictures of family life (a Victorian obsession). Most of the pictures are of dysfunctional families in a tragic mode; here we find the same phenomenon in a comic mode.

For Reflection or Discussion

What are the sources of humor in the chapter? How does the information about Miss Havisham cast light on action up to this point? What information carries a tag "to be continued?" A story is always revealing of the person who composed it; at this point in your journey through *Great Expectations*, what is your impression of Dickens as a person?

There is no better introduction to things British than *Great Expectations*. On Pip's first Sunday in London, he and Herbert "went to church at Westminster Abbey, and in the afternoon we walked in the Parks." This is what any tourist in London might do, and we can profitably reflect on the ways in which Pip shares important qualities with a tourist during his first few days in London.

CHAPTER 23

Dinner at the Pocket House

Plot Summary

The last third of the preceding chapter had transferred Pip from his apartment to the Pocket residence in a suburb, and this chapter is the sequel, narrating what happened as the visit gradually moved toward the evening meal. First we get a fuller picture of Mr. and Mrs. Pocket. A neighbor, Mrs. Coiler, adds still more mirth to the account. The Pocket children are on their usual terrible behavior, Herbert's apartment acquaintance Drummle is likewise his usual terrible self, and the crowning touch comes when at the end of the evening the cook lies "insensibly drunk on the kitchen floor, with a large bundle of fresh butter made up in the cupboard ready to sell for grease." Who but Dickens could produce this chapter?

Commentary

The first thing to note is that this chapter, too, is a comic masterpiece. Some of the comedy resides in the characters, such as the incompetent Mrs. Pocket with her aspirations to be aristocratic, or the "toady neighbour" Mrs. Coiler, who (as her name states) smothers everyone with unwanted flattery and attention. There is also situation comedy in abundance, as when Mr. Pocket stands up at the meal, pulls his hair upward, and "exclaimed to the elements, 'Hear this. . . . Babies are to be nutcrackered dead, for people's poor grandpapa's positions!' Then he let himself down again, and became silent." The final note in the chapter combines situation comedy and comedy of character: "Mr. Pocket . . . dropped upon [the sofa] in the attitude of the Dying Gladiator. Still in that attitude he said, with a hollow voice, 'Good night, Mr. Pip.'"

In addition to relishing the comedy, we need to keep the story of Pip's initiation in view. In the visit to the Pocket house, Pip is writing another chapter in what is supposed to be a "brave new world" of excitement and improvement. More specifically, the hapless Mrs. Pocket, hankering to be a high society sophisticate, represents the very dream that Pip is ready to pursue.

Early in this guide we noted some of the things that make up the quality of being "good at characterization." The list includes the creation of universal character types, the invention of unique (one of a kind) characters, and the satiric knack for creating characters who embody foibles of character that are (in Dickens's case) gently held up to ridicule. This chapter is rich in these characters.

For Reflection or Discussion

One avenue toward appreciation is the comedy that Dickens packs into this chapter. Second, in the Pocket family and other characters who parade in front of us, we can see an abundance of real-life experiences (we can never remind ourselves too often that the subject of literature is universal human experience). Finally, all that happens in this chapter (and the ensuing ones) is part of Pip's pursuit of his great expectations; exactly how great are they?

CHAPTER 24

Getting to Know Mr. Jaggers

Plot Summary

This is another chapter devoted to Pip's assimilation into his new life in London. What transpires is close to our own experience of settling into a dorm room on campus or into an apartment after graduation from college. Pip requests money from Mr. Jaggers to buy furniture, and Jaggers's clerk Wemmick gives him the money on the spot. From this initial transaction in Mr. Jaggers's law office we branch out to Pip's fuller introduction to Mr. Jaggers and his law practice.

Pip accepts Wemmick's offer to be shown around the offices, and what Pip sees proves unsettling. The main feature is the clay-cast heads of famous clients. Mr. Jaggers's success is obvious, but there is also an air of his being a bully. Everyone fears him. Before the chapter ends, Pip has been invited to spend an overnight at the home of Wemmick at some future date, and a sense of

There is something dreamlike and surreal about Jaggers and his legal practice. What is one to make of a law office with a display case of cast heads of former clients? Dickens does not make an explicit denunciation of Jaggers, yet a literary critic claims that Jaggers's "trade is the perversion of justice. His tools are bullying and deception, and he uses them with deft legality."

suspense arises when Wemmick informs Pip that when he dines at Mr. Jaggers's he will see a very special housekeeper—"a wild beast tamed." We have no way of knowing what this means, but our curiosity is piqued.

Commentary

With a great storyteller like Dickens, two stories are often being told at the same time—the surface story and the deeper story. The ostensible plotline is the further initiation of Pip in his life of great expectations. If Pip is to make a good life for himself in the city, he needs furniture for his apartment. Mr. Jaggers is his guardian and the dispenser of money from the anonymous benefactor. It is entirely natural that Pip finds himself in Jaggers's law office.

But once we enter that office with Pip, more subtle lines of action begin to unfold. First, we suddenly become immersed in a world of law, crime, courts, legal defense, and people's lives being determined by the judicial system. Dickens is a social critic, and before the novel is finished he will make indictments of the judicial system of Victorian England. We catch hints of the perversion of justice already in this chapter. Second, Jaggers is another one of Dickens's memorable character creations, and we get to know him somewhat better in this chapter. Additionally, Jaggers represents success and power, and those are the very things that Pip hopes to achieve. But as Pip the first-person narrator conveys the information of this chapter, we can sense a degree of revulsion against Jaggers.

For Reflection or Discussion

What are the signs of success around Jaggers's law office? How is his employee Wemmick an exten-

Victorian England worshiped material prosperity and success. Jaggers worships power and money. A good label for this cluster of values is "the success ethic." It is given memorable expression throughout the novel in Wemmick's famous epithet "portable property," meaning money. In this chapter he advises Pip, "Get hold of portable property."

sion of this devotion to success and power? If we look closely and "read between the lines," what can we say about Pip's assessment of what he encounters at Jaggers's law office?

CHAPTER 25
Getting to Know Wemmick

Plot Summary

It is only natural that Pip would be in the process of getting to know the people who are part of his new life in London, and of course we get to know them along with Pip. First we are given just a little more information about Bentley Drummle, who is "sulky" and sinister. As in real life, one's new acquaintances are not all likeable. The bulk of the chapter is then devoted to Wemmick. Pip spends a night at Wemmick's residence, which is so unique that it is hard to believe the details. The eccentricity of the house is typically British. Also British is the separation of the domestic sphere from the public one, and the index to this comes at the end when "by degrees, Wemmick got dryer and harder as we went along [to the office the next morning], and his mouth tightened into a post-office again."

Although this chapter is devoted to Wemmick rather than Jaggers, we learn an important thing about Jaggers, namely, that he never locks his house and has never been robbed. Wemmick ascribes it to the "dread" that people feel toward Jaggers. Certainly Jaggers is one of Dickens's most colorful character creations.

Commentary

Dickens is always inventive, and the details that he imagines for Wemmick's home elicit his creativity to a remarkable degree. Of course we are expected to find humor in the details. The formula "vintage British" is very relevant. First, it is a British saying that "a man's house is his castle," and we get a literal version of it here (inasmuch as the house is built like a tiny castle). Then there is the British impulse toward being individualistic and idiosyncratic; Wemmick fits that description. But his private life is kept out of sight from the public, and Dickens makes it clear that Jaggers (Wemmick's employer, no less) knows nothing about this domestic life of his employee, and we are told at the end that by the time Wemmick enters the office "he looked as unconscious of his Walworth property as if the Castle and drawbridge . . . had been blown into space. . . ."

Wemmick informs Pip that Jaggers, his employer, knows nothing about his domestic routine. As an extension of that, Wemmick explains that "when I go into the office, I leave the Castle behind me, and when I come into the Castle, I leave the office behind me." Wemmick then requests Pip to do the same. The mindset here is typically British, as is virtually everything else about *Great Expectations*.

For Reflection or Discussion

What elements of foreshadowing can you tease out of the opening description of Drummle? What are your favorite details in regard to Wemmick's one-of-a-kind residence? Pip's initiation into Wemmick's domestic routine invites comparison with what Pip found during his visit to the Pocket home; what parallels and contrasts do you detect?

CHAPTER 26

Dinner at Mr. Jaggers's House

Plot Summary

Wemmick has by this time made several anticipatory comments about what it will be like when Pip has dinner at Mr. Jaggers's house, and now that the time has arrived, we experience it as something very special. We learn that Jaggers has the habit of conducting a ritual washing after he has dealt with a client, and if the client is really bad, Jaggers also gargles. On the day of the dinner at his house, Pip finds Jaggers in his office cleaning his nails as well!

Pip's senses are heightened as he records what happened at Jaggers's house. Four young men from Pip's apartment building have been invited to the meal (the same four that had dinner at the Pockets'). Drummle, "the blotchy, sprawly, sulky fellow," as Jaggers calls him, plays a prominent role. His behavior at the table is "downright intolerable," and Jaggers nicknames him the Spider. But given the kind of power broker that Jaggers himself is, there is a logic to Jaggers's telling Pip at the end of the evening, "I like the fellow." As the group is ready to leave for the evening, Pip runs back for a parting word with Jaggers and finds him "already hard at it, washing his hands of us." We naturally draw a connection between the gang of four and Jaggers's offensive clients.

Although Jaggers's housemaid gets only minor space, the importance that we attach to her is disproportionate to that small space. Jaggers showcases the woman's strength of arm and wrist. We also see (along with Pip) that the woman is "much disfigured—deeply scarred and scarred across and across." All we can conclude from this minimal information is something to the effect of "stay tuned."

Commentary

It is a truism of storytelling that a house is an extension of the owner's personality and character. We have seen this with Wemmick's tiny castle and its routines. Now we see it with Mr. Jaggers's house in Soho. The same thing is true of the rituals of mealtime and hospitality. In real life, as on this visit, we do not know exactly what to make of all that we see the first time we visit a person's home, but we intuitively sense that some of what we are seeing carries a hidden meaning.

Being invited to someone's house for the evening meal has now become an established part of London life for Pip. It is reminiscent of the attention to meals and eating in Homer's *Odyssey*. By the time we have attended all of these meals with Pip, we have a rather complete picture of Victorian etiquette and rituals in regard to dinner entertainment. But of course we need to ponder their relevance to Pip's development as well.

The characterization of Jaggers is important in this episode. His authoritarianism and controlling nature are strongly reinforced. He himself serves the courses of the meal and hands out clean plates and utensils. He draws attention to his maid's strength of wrist. He announces that his guests must leave at 9:30 and directs them to "make the best use of your time" until then. He delights in the intolerable bully Drummle.

Drummle seems to receive an arbitrary importance in this chapter. But storytellers are the ones to decide what is relevant and important. One of the functions of literature is to give expression to our own fears and dislikes; Drummle surely embodies what we dislike in his behavior at the meal. What is merely obnoxious behavior here will escalate into villainy as the story unfolds.

For Reflection or Discussion

What details of the visit to Jaggers's house are most noteworthy to you? What are the elements of humor? How is the characterization of Jaggers confirmed and extended? What elements of foreshadowing do you detect (even though obviously we do not know exactly what it is that is being foreshadowed)? It is also appropriate to take stock of the block of chapters devoted to Pip's arrival and first days in London; Pip has been like the utopian visitor in fictional utopias, recording his observations and being alternately excited and bewildered by what he encounters. What stands out as most noteworthy?

CHAPTER 27

Joe Visits Pip in London

Plot Summary

For seven chapters our attention has been directed so single-mindedly to Pip's round of activities and new relationships in London that we have all but forgotten about life in the village where Pip was raised. That amnesia is brought to a sudden end in this chapter when Joe sends a letter announcing that he will visit Pip (the letter is actually written by Biddy on behalf of Joe). Pip is embarrassed by the prospect of Joe's visit. Joe arrives and is ill at ease throughout his conversation with Pip in the latter's apartment. The most important aspect of the visit is that Joe informs Pip that Miss Havisham wishes to see him, and that Estella has come home and "would be glad to see him."

Commentary

One of the great strengths of this novel is the variety provided by the two worlds that Dickens creates—the world of the small town and the world of London. Pip's recent life has been a whirl of activities—life in the fast lane in the big city. The intrusion of the hometown village back into Pip's life is something of a reality check. The most important aspect of this chapter is the developing characterization of Pip. His embarrassment over Joe's visit and inability to see that he is making Joe feel awkward during the visit are an index to Pip's snobbishness and feeling of urban superiority over the simple man from the small town. In a similar vein, in the early part of the chapter Pip rehearses some details of his extravagant lifestyle, seen (for example) in his perpetually decorating his living quarters and hiring a servant.

Dickens is at heart a comic writer, and he fills this chapter with comic touches. Having hired and outfitted a houseman, Pip finds it a trial to find work for him—so much so that he nicknames him "The Avenger"! Joe's hat keeps falling from its perch on the chimney piece. Joe's erratic behavior at mealtime is hilarious, and the details of his dress for the visit are "insoluble mysteries" to Pip.

As always, it is how Dickens expresses himself that creates the humor in the events he narrates. There are a dozen or more examples in this chapter. Here is what happens at mealtime, for example: Joe "fell into such unaccountable fits of meditation, with his fork midway between his plate and his mouth; had his eyes attracted in such strange directions; was afflicted with such remarkable coughs; sat so far from the table and dropped so much more than he ate, and pretended that he hadn't dropped it."

The last paragraph of this chapter is remarkable and compels us to interpret its meaning. Pip observes as Joe leaves that "there was a simple dignity in him," and after coming to that conclusion Pip "hurried out after him and looked for him in the neighbouring streets." Why?

These are only specimens of the humor that permeates this chapter.

For Reflection or Discussion

What developments in Pip's characterization occur? In effect we are allowed to catch our breath after the breakneck speed of the preceding seven chapters devoted to Pip's initiation into the "big time" life of the city; what have been the effects on Pip? What comic details are presented for our amusement? What meanings do you extract from the concluding paragraph?

CHAPTER 28

Journey to the Village

Plot Summary

In a long narrative like a novel, it is customary for a detail that is planted late in a chapter to propel us into the next chapter, where the foreshadowed event becomes the central action. The last notable piece of information that Joe had imparted to Pip in the preceding chapter was that Miss Havisham and Estella wished to see him, so this chapter is devoted to Pip's journey from London to "Hometown." Dickens springs a surprise on us: instead of narrating a pleasant and nostalgic journey to the village, most of the space is given to the presence of two handcuffed convicts on the coach who are being transported to the convict ships on the marsh. To deepen Pip's discomfort, one of the two convicts is the man who in an earlier scene had stirred his rum with Joe's file and given Pip reward money for having helped the convict in the graveyard.

Commentary

Although Pip had begun to think of himself as finished with his life in the village of his upbringing, and to think that he would no longer have contact with the criminal element of society, he is now brought back into an encounter with those very things. It is as though Pip is contaminated by his proximity to the two convicts in the coach. There is also an element of suspense in the coach ride, inasmuch as Pip fears that the rum-stirring criminal from the pub might recognize him.

When Pip springs clear from the coach and settles down to the comfort of the Blue Boar Inn, we experience a sense of relief with him. But then we are unsettled by another unexpected invention from Dickens: Pip finds in a copy of the local newspaper that Uncle Pumblechook had written a piece claiming to be Pip's benefactor! In case we had begun to think of the city as the only repository of pretentiousness and fraud, this detail alerts us to their universality.

For Reflection or Discussion

A good analytic strategy is to theorize about why an author invented the material that he or she places before us. Alternatively, we can think of the matter in terms of theorizing about the effect of the author having done it. In this chapter, what is the effect of the emphasis on the convicts and the criminal's life? Why does Dickens make one of the two convicts the same one who had delivered money to Pip in the earlier scene set in the pub? Why does Dickens invent the detail of Uncle Pumblechook's publicly claiming to be Pip's anonymous benefactor?

It is a rule of storytelling that a correspondence exists between an external setting and the action that takes place within and the characters that inhabit it. The two main characters on the coach are criminals, and as they talk we come to inhabit their criminal world. Dickens multiplies the negative features of the landscape, the weather, and the marshes. It all reaches a climax when Pip imagines the convicts' arrival at the convict ship (which he labels "a wicked Noah's Ark") with the "convict crew waiting for them at the slime-washed stairs" of a boat "lying out on the black water." At some level this chapter narrates a journey into inferno (Dante would have loved the boat-side scene and may have influenced Dickens in his composition of it).

CHAPTER 29

A Strange Meeting at Miss Havisham's House

Plot Summary

The action in this chapter is a surrealistic convergence of mysterious and unlikely events. The chapter has a dreamlike quality about it, and no matter how many times we read it, we are left feeling that we have not quite understood everything. The main action is Pip's visit to Miss Havisham's house, where Estella and Jaggers are also present. We encounter an initial shock along with Pip when the new porter at the gate of the house turns out to be the villainous Orlick.

Thereafter the chapter unfolds in six scenes. First Pip interacts with Miss Havisham and Estella. Estella is completely transformed from the last time we saw her. She is a beautiful and elegant young lady. There are hints that Miss Havisham is manipulating Estella for a purpose; for example, she asks Pip, "Do you find her much changed, Pip?" Second, after it is decided that Pip will spend the day at the house, he and Estella leave the house for a conversation in the decaying garden that we had encountered early in the novel. Estella remains contemptuous of Pip and also informs him that she has "no heart" and is incapable of feeling. It is apparent that Pip remains as much in love with Estella as ever.

Third, when Estella and Pip return to the house at dinnertime, no other than Jaggers has become part of the group, visiting Miss Havisham for a business matter. In a return to the manipulative mode, Miss Havisham tells Pip repeatedly, "Love

One of the overall strategies of this novel is to build up Pip's great expectations and then to deflate them. This chapter develops both of those motifs. On the one hand, Pip's imagination runs wild with pictures of a glorious future with Estella at his side and Miss Havisham financing his lifestyle. Subverting that are the many details in this chapter that return Pip and us to his roots in the village. There are hints that Pip's great expectations are an illusion.

her, love her, love her. How does she use you?" Fourth, this strange group sits down to dinner together, with Jaggers the domineering presence. Then fifth, in an equally surrealistic development, Pip and Estella play cards in front of Miss Havisham until nine o'clock. The chapter is rounded out with a sixth scene back at the Blue Boar Inn. As Pip lies in his bed, he is overwhelmed with gratitude that Estella has been destined to be his beloved.

Commentary

To make sense of the details of this mysterious chapter, we need to stand back at a distance and get a grip on three big principles for this story as a whole. First, the whole story is based on a contrast between two worlds. One is the world of the village and of Pip as "the blacksmith's boy" (as Pip calls himself in his reverie in the hotel room at the end of the chapter). The other is the world of privilege in London—the world of Pip's great expectations. Those two worlds collide in this chapter. In particular, after the excitement and unreality of Pip's life as a gentleman in London, this chapter is filled with ties to the past: Miss Havisham and her house, Sarah Pocket, Orlick, and the town itself (including Miss Havisham's house and the Blue Boar Inn). Multiple meanings reside in this forced return of Pip and to his humble roots.

Secondly, it is important to the understanding of this novel that it is at one level a love story. In the second paragraph of this chapter, Pip tells us that he "loved Estella with the love of a man" and that he loved her "simply because I found her irresistible." In this chapter, with its conspicuous emphasis on Estella's emerging beauty, the love motif receives major development.

Consistently the concluding paragraphs of the chapters in this novel pack a punch and cast an interpretive light on what has happened in the chapter. The concluding note in this chapter is Pip's remorse over his not having made contact with Joe because he knew that the glamorous Estella "would be contemptuous of him." In fact, Pip prays, "God forgive me" (observe the Christian frame of reference) for the fact that his tears of remorse "soon dried."

Thirdly, the mystery of Pip's benefactor is one of the big concerns of a story that (as we need continuously to remind ourselves) is a mystery story and detective thriller. A suspense story requires that we follow false leads. This chapter is loaded with dramatic irony: everything seems to confirm Pip's conclusion that Miss Havisham is his benefactor and that she intends Estella as his beloved. A major thrust of the middle part of *Great Expectations* is that Pip builds an entire life based on false premises. This chapter fits into that pattern in a major way.

For Reflection or Discussion

What details in the chapter put Pip back in touch with his roots in the village? What do you conclude Dickens intends with this strategy? What details fit into the romantic love interest in the story?

CHAPTER 30

Return to London

Plot Summary

This chapter is a follow-up and sequel to the preceding one. After the intensity of the happenings at Miss Havisham's house, this is a "sit down" chapter in which Pip interprets what has happened in a conversation with Herbert Pocket back at Barnard's Inn (Pip's apartment in London). Before returning us to London, however, Dickens invents one of his great comic scenes as Trabb's boy (the employee of the clothing store owner Trabb), jealous of Pip's wealth and life of privilege, mocks him on High Street (British for American "Main Street"). Later, back at the apartment, Pip shares his conviction that Estella is intended for him. Herbert sounds a note of caution regarding Estella and even asks Pip if he could give up his infatuation with her. At the end of the conversation we learn that Herbert is engaged to Clara, who cares for her invalid father.

Commentary

The scene of mockery in which Trabb's boy darts in and out of sight provides what literary critics call comic relief—a scene that gets our minds off of oppressive issues and diverts us with humor. The conversation between Herbert and Pip serves at least three functions. (1) It reinforces Pip's conviction (eventually disproved) that he will marry Estella as part of his inheritance from his benefactor (mistakenly thought by Pip to be Miss Havisham). (2) The cautions that Herbert raises about Estella are a device of disclosure that pushes us as readers (though not Pip as a participant) toward a premonition that Pip's great expectations are beset with potential tragedy. (3) The introduction of Clara Barley (we later learn her last name) as Herbert's fiancée. She is an addition to a group of couples who will be married before the novel is finished, which in turn embodies a Victorian preoccupation with romantic love and domestic values.

For Reflection or Discussion

What moments of comedy do you particularly relish in the opening scene of mockery? What danger signs emerge in regard to Pip's future in the conversation between Pip and Herbert? Stated another way, at what moments during the conversation do you have premonitions that Pip is basing his exuberance on false premises?

A comic scene like the mockery that Trabb's boy heaps on Pip needs to be relished for its humor. It is a "stand alone" in that regard. But everything in this novel ties into the announced focus of "great expectations." Pip's being rendered ridiculous by Trabb's boy hints at the truth that in his pretentiousness and snobbishness he is, in fact, ridiculous.

Although this novel was published serially (in installments in Dickens's magazine *All the Year Round*), it is again obvious that Dickens had the whole story worked out in marvelous detail right from the start. Late in this chapter we read the seemingly insignificant detail that Clara's father formerly worked in the food supply of passenger ships (presumably on the Thames River). This will eventually play an important role when Pip attempts to smuggle someone out of London by boat.

CHAPTER 31

Mr. Wopsle's Acting Career

Plot Summary

This chapter is strictly an interlude. In an earlier chapter we learned in a passing comment during Joe's visit that Mr. Wopsle had left the employment of the church back in the village and had moved to London to pursue an acting career. This chapter fills out what that means as Pip and Herbert attend a performance of Shakespeare's *Hamlet* in which Mr. Wopsle performs. The chapter adheres to the literary genre known as the burlesque—the comically exaggerated. We are given an exaggerated account of the ineptitude of the actors who perform *Hamlet*. After the performance, Mr. Wopsle visits Pip and Herbert in their apartment, rehearsing his past and hoped-for career in the theater until two in the morning.

Commentary

On the surface, this chapter is a comic interlude, as we are treated to a hilarious and improbable spectacle of theatrical ineptitude. The poorness of the acting is so exaggerated that we can barely catch a glimpse of Shakespeare's play. Comic effect is what Dickens creates. But of course in a masterpiece like this, governed by an impressive unity, it is natural to ask how it fits into the serious thematic purpose of the novel. The motif of great expectations holds the clue to this level of meaning. Like Pip, Mr. Wopsle has great expectations in regard to his acting career; in fact, he aims at the "reviving of Drama." He is actually part of an enterprise that is ridiculous from start

As noted in the accompanying plot summary, one genre at work in this chapter is the burlesque. The label of parody is also accurate: the imitation of a literary work in such a way that the effect of the original text is distorted or actually inverted. As Dickens gives us a summary of the inept performance of *Hamlet*, Shakespeare's great tragedy is reduced to a comic farce.

As usual, the last paragraph of the chapter packs the punch. Pip goes to bed miserable, and (more importantly) "miserably dreamed that my expectations were all cancelled."

to finish. Might Pip be engaged in something as futile as this?

For Reflection or Discussion

The spectacle of ineptitude gains its full effect only if we are familiar with Shakespeare's *Hamlet*; if you have that familiarity, what connections do you make between the play and the exaggerated lack of skill that Dickens imagines for this chapter? If you are inclined to make a connection between Mr. Wopsle's acting career and Pip's pretensions at greatness as an affluent gentleman, what are those connections?

CHAPTER 32

Visit to Newgate Prison

Plot Summary

The chapter begins with a sensational piece of information: a letter from Estella informs Pip that she will be passing through London in three days and wishes to meet Pip. But the visit is deferred until the next chapter. With time on his hands, Pip accepts Wemmick's invitation to visit Newgate Prison with him. We then receive an account of the legal business that Wemmick transacts with various people in the prison, in language that is often technical. As they leave the prison, Wemmick speaks in a tone of awe about Jaggers's immense power in the judicial world of which we have caught a glimpse in this chapter.

Storytellers love to move back and forth between extremes. The technical term is juxtaposition. The preceding chapter paraded a spectacle of total lack of professional expertise before us in the form of the bad performance of *Hamlet*. This chapter treats us to a picture of complete professional expertise in the form of Wemmick's control of his legal routine.

Commentary

There are three main things that capture our attention—the renewed evidence of the importance of crime and criminals to this story, the details that occur in the prison as Wemmick interacts with inmates, and Pip's response to the visit at the end of the chapter. As for the first of these, it is a fact that from the opening chapter of this novel to very late in it, the action joins two marginalized and even abused groups within Victorian society—the child and the criminal. Additionally, even though we do not know it on a first reading, Pip's anonymous benefactor is a criminal. In a sense, therefore, in visiting the prison Pip unknowingly enters the world that is financing his lifestyle and fuelling his great expectations.

Secondly, it is obvious from Wemmick's interaction with the prisoners in their cells that as Jaggers's emissary he is a master of the legal and judicial world represented by the prison. He "walked among the prisoners, much as a gardener might walk among his plants." Wemmick is thoroughly familiar with his clients' situations and the legal strategies that Jaggers intends regarding their cases. Along with Pip, we are perplexed and made uneasy by the intimacy and power that Wemmick and Jaggers possess in regard to the criminal element of society.

Finally (and predictably at the end of the chapter) Pip tells us how he feels about his visit. When confronted with evidence of Jaggers's absolute power in the legal and judicial world, Pip wishes that he "had some other guardian of minor abilities." Second, Pip was "consumed the whole time in thinking how strange it was that I should be encompassed by all this taint of prison and crime." Little does he know. . . . Third, Pip is led to think "of the beautiful young Estella, proud and refined, coming towards me, and I thought with absolute

In Pip's musings at the end of the chapter, Dickens in effect highlights the motif of Pip's connection with the criminal world. Pip reflects how "strange it was" that he had first encountered this world in the churchyard and that "it should have reappeared on two occasions" (the rum-stirring visitor in the pub and the handcuffed criminal breathing down his neck on the coach ride to the village). Not only that: Pip compares it to a stain that keeps reappearing and shares his obsessions with how "it should in this new way pervade his fortune and advancement." Again we can say, little does Pip know what is in store for him in regard to contact with a criminal.

abhorrence of the contrast between the jail and her." Finally, that abhorrence is so intense that Pip "beat the prison dust off [his] feet" and "exhaled its air from [his] lungs."

For Reflection or Discussion

It is the function of literature to re-create places and events with such vividness that we vicariously live the experiences that the author places before us. If Pip experiences the visit to the prison first-hand, so do we as readers. It is profitable to ask what *our* responses are to the details of the visit. We can then compare them to the responses that Pip shares at the end of the chapter. Finally, we need to reach some provisional conclusions regarding why Dickens makes Pip's contact with the criminal world so prominent in the novel.

CHAPTER 33

Meeting Estella in London

Plot Summary

The anticipated visit of Estella is the subject of this chapter. She looks "delicately beautiful" in "her furred travelling-dress." Estella plays the role know in literary terms as the coquette—the attractive female who plays hard to get and teases men with her unattainable charms. Flirtation is part of the arsenal for such a female. In this chapter, Estella leads Pip on, letting him kiss her on the cheek but "gliding away the instant [he] touched her cheek." Pip accompanies Estella by coach to the London suburb of Richmond, where she is to live in style with a wealthy lady.

A main strand in this chapter is the nature of Pip's infatuation with the beautiful and glamorous Estella. The key to the relationship at this point is that Pip's love is not portrayed as ignoble; it is Estella who is ignoble. A key statement is Pip's awareness that "I never was happy with her, but always miserable." Pip's infatuation could turn into a happy romance if Estella were to become worthy of Pip's love. (Stay tuned.)

Commentary

A lot is going on beneath the surface. First, Estella in her finery, headed for the genteel life in a wealthy home in Richmond, represents what Pip, too, aspires toward. As readers we can scarcely avoid seeing how unworthy that life is. Second, the romantic love motif remains in high gear in this chapter, as Pip remains totally infatuated with Estella. In regard to this, we need always to remember that storytellers begin with matters in one position and end them in the opposite position. At the end of the story Pip will win the love of Estella, but only after she has been changed by suffering and become worthy of Pip's love. At this point she is unworthy of Pip's adoration, but we should avoid reaching any final conclusion in the matter.

For Reflection or Discussion

As you get to know Estella more fully in this chapter, what kind of person do you take her to be? What clues are there that she is not a simple character? Equally, we need to draw conclusions about Pip's development as a character in this chapter. What things are reinforced? What is added to his developing portrait?

After depositing Estella at the house in Richmond, Pip returns to his apartment to find "little Jane Pocket coming to our home from a little party escorted by her little lover." It is a semi-humorous portrait, of course, but in a telling addition, Pip confides that he "envied her little lover." In a touch of humor, we learn that Mr. Pocket, head of a completely dysfunctional family, has become a well-known lecturer on how to run a household and is the author of acclaimed "treatises on the management of children and servants."

CHAPTER 34

Pip as Spendthrift

Plot Summary

The account in this chapter of Pip's overspending to finance his extravagant lifestyle returns us to the plotline of Pip's great expectations as a London gentleman. It is as though we had returned to the earlier block of chapters devoted to narrating Pip's first days in London. The opening subordinate clause introduces the motif: "As I had grown accustomed to my expectations. . . ." Dickens's assessment of this life is negative, and he accordingly chooses to satirize Pip in this chapter by rendering his experiment in living ridiculous. An aspect of this satire is the account of how Pip and Herbert join a club called The Finches of the Grove, which fosters the foolish spending of money on expensive meals.

The keynote of the chapter is the effect on Pip's and Herbert's lives of their overspending. Their lives become "always more or less miserable." Pip pays Herbert visits in his dingy office to escape boredom. The masterpiece of the account is the humorous account of the rituals they develop for tallying up their debts. The practice is euphemistically called "looking into our affairs." The ritual begins with ordering something special for dinner, followed by a frenzy of paperwork. Under a pretense of "looking the thing in the face," the pair actually avoids coming to grips with the seriousness of their debts. The chapter ends with the typical storytelling device of something that propels us into the next chapter—an announcement of the death of Joe's wife (Pip's sister) Mrs. Gargery.

The opening paragraph is devoted to an exploration of Pip's conscience. It turns out that under the whirl of activities that makes up his life of privilege Pip bears a guilty conscience regarding his repudiation of his humble origins, especially in regard to his relations with Biddy and Joe. Virtually everything in this novel relates to the announced theme of great expectations.

Throughout the middle section of the book, the story of Pip's great expectations has a double thrust: on the one hand life in the fast lane is very exciting, but on the other, it fails to satisfy and is accompanied by Pip's awareness that he is pursuing a dead end.

Commentary

This chapter is a typical Dickensian blend of the serious and the comic. We begin with the serious reflection about Pip's "weariness of spirits," about how he wishes he "had never seen Miss Havisham's face," and about how, as he looked into the fire of his room, he "thought, after all, there was no fire like the forge fire and the kitchen fire at home." This sets a keynote for a chapter that exposes the shallowness of Pip's life of luxury.

We had been lulled into the impression that Pip's allotment of money from his benefactor was limitless, but we now share Pip's anxiety as we learn that he has run up a hopeless debt. But Dickens's style is often to treat serious matters with humor, and Pip's ritual for tallying up his debts is handled in the comic mode. The accounting process is accompanied with such a show of expertise and method that Pip states (to our amusement) that on these occasions he established with himself (!) "the reputation of a first-rate man of business—prompt, decisive, energetic, clear, cool-headed." There is additional satiric humor in the practice of "leaving a Margin," creating the appearance that the pair has more money than appears from their statement of debt.

Herbert serves as a foil (parallel) to Pip in regard to the theme of great expectations. When Pip first met him, he expressed grandiose dreams of "looking about" and then "swooping" on the opportunity when it suddenly presented itself. The fact is that Herbert has an insignificant job in a dark back room. Both Herbert's and Pip's dreams of an affluent life are without a firm foundation.

For Reflection or Discussion

What elements of humor enliven the chapter? What details lead us to see that Dickens is managing the account in such a way as to make us critical of Pip's lifestyle?

CHAPTER 35

The Funeral in the Village

Plot Summary

True to the narrative principle of juxtaposition of contrasting material, in this chapter we move to something very different from Pip tallying up his debts in his apartment. We are transported to

"Hometown" for the funeral of Joe's sister. Dickens chooses to treat the funeral in a comic mode. A high point of humor comes when Pip describes the people in the funeral procession leaving the home with "pocket-handkerchiefs to our faces, as if our noses were bleeding," and filing out "two and two." But there are many other comic touches as well.

The second half of the chapter recounts the "cold dinner" that Joe, Biddy, and Pip have at home on the evening of the funeral. After dinner Pip and Biddy have a conversation in the adjoining garden. Pip learns the tear-jerking details of his sister's last moments and about how the villainous Orlick still bothers Biddy. Unpleasantness ensues over Biddy's addressing Pip as "Mr. Pip," and over the skepticism that Biddy expresses when Pip claims he will come to visit Joe often and regularly.

Commentary

The main motif is the difficulty that Pip displays in relating to the people back home. The ridiculous details of the funeral show that the city has no "corner" on pretentiousness, a human propensity that shows itself in full force in the village as well. By contrast, when for the evening meal Joe Gargery replaces his Sunday clothes with his best ordinary clothes, we read that "the dear fellow looked natural, and like the Man he was." The main point of the unpleasantness between Pip and Biddy is to accentuate the bad influence on Pip of his new lifestyle in the city. This is confirmed by the concluding paragraph in which Pip indicts himself for not following through on his stated intention to visit Joe on a regular basis.

Pip's behavior in the chapter is ambivalent. He is moved to indignation at Orlick's harassment of Biddy. He recognizes the inherent dignity of Joe and Biddy's humble life of the kitchen. He is repelled by the hollow rituals surrounding the funeral. But on the other hand he is self-congratulatory about asking Joe to allow him to sleep in his "own little room," he is waspish toward Biddy for no good reason, and he makes a rash promise to visit Joe often that Pip knows he will not keep.

The final paragraph begins, "Once more, the mists were rising as I walked away." The mists and their rising are a unifying image pattern in this novel and will make a notable appearance in the book's conclusion.

For Reflection or Discussion

How does the motif of pretentiousness or "putting on airs" work itself out in this chapter? What details show Pip to be a divided soul?

CHAPTER 36

Pip Turns Twenty-One

Plot Summary

Pip informs us that he and Herbert engaged in "a crowd of speculations and anticipations" as they looked toward Pip's coming-of-age (turning twenty-one). In fact, they had entertained the hope that Jaggers as guardian would say "something definite on that occasion." On his birthday, Pip arrives at Little Britain (the street on which Jaggers's law office is located) and is extravagantly congratulated by his guardian. Jaggers repeatedly refuses to disclose the name of Pip's benefactor or predict when that person will come to London. Instead he gives Pip a five-hundred-pound banknote.

Jaggers accepts an invitation to dine at Barnard's Inn (Pip's apartment), and while he is winding things up in the office, Pip talks to Wemmick in his room. He takes Wemmick into his confidence that he wishes to use the money he has been given to help a friend. Wemmick scorns investing "portable property [money] in a friend." Wemmick makes a distinction between his official viewpoint of the law office and his personal opinions at Walworth (his home), so a visit is scheduled for Pip at Walworth. Jaggers's visit to the apartment leaves Pip and Herbert depressed.

Most of the chapters in part 2 of the novel (the chapters devoted to Pip's life as a gentleman) contain short passages (called "asides" when they appear in a drama) that function as a background chorus of moral sentiment that stands as a contrast to Pip's active devotion to the success ethic. The final paragraph in this chapter is such a passage of moral commentary. In it, both Pip and Herbert express their distaste for the powerful Jaggers.

Commentary

This chapter is chiefly important for the plot. Pip's coming into an extra sum of money will prove important when he uses it to set Herbert up in business. Jaggers's refusal to disclose the identity of Pip's benefactor perpetuates the mystery surrounding it. Pip's characterization is a secondary interest, as we infer a generous spirit in his desire "to serve a friend."

For Reflection or Discussion

As is often the case with Dickens, the way to read a chapter like this is not so much to find out *what* happens but to relish *how* Dickens expresses that information. How does the concluding paragraph underscore an important moral emphasis of the story?

CHAPTER 37

A Second Visit to Wemmick's House

Plot Summary

We have already paid one visit to Wemmick's unusual residence, and now we are treated to a second visit. Two main events occur. First, Pip is invited to meet Wemmick's girlfriend named Miss Skiffins. Secondly, Pip follows through on his plan to donate money to set Herbert up in the shipping business.

The Victorian era venerated the institutions of home and family. One index to this preoccupation in *Great Expectations* is the number of couples who get married by the end of the novel. We have already been introduced to Herbert and Clara. Now Wemmick and Miss Skiffins are on our radar screen.

Commentary

Any account of a visit to Wemmick's one-of-a-kind "castle" is lively, and this chapter does not disappoint. Additionally, Miss Skiffins takes on a life of her own and is one of Dickens's great character inventions. In Dickens's works, the first description of a character is often a classic; in the case of Miss Skiffins, we are told that she "was of a wooden appearance" and someone whom Pip judged "to stand possessed of portable property." The account of Wemmick's attempts to put his arm around his girlfriend's waist as an expression of affection is likewise a small classic.

The event of setting Herbert up in business is a major ingredient in the plot, though we do not yet know the extent of that significance. But even without the fuller picture at our disposal, we catch a hint of the significance of the event when Pip confides that he cried when he went to bed "to think that my expectations had done some good to somebody."

Heretofore Pip has used his money frivolously and self-indulgently. Here we see moral growth as Pip is generous with his money as an expression of friendship to Herbert.

For Reflection or Discussion

First we need to relish the humor with which Dickens manages the details of Wemmick's domestic routine and his relationship with Miss Skiffins. Then we need to assess what moral statement is made by Pip's generosity with his money and his friendship toward Herbert. Although we do not yet know it, this is the last chapter in the novel in which Pip still has great expectations, so we need to take stock of how we evaluate Pip's character development under the influence of money and privilege. Exactly how bad has his character become?

CHAPTER 38

Bad News Regarding Estella

Plot Summary

At the end of the preceding chapter, Pip had said that before telling us about the turning point of his life (as narrated two chapters later) he "must give one chapter to Estella." Chapter 38 is that chapter. We first learn that Estella, living in Richmond, "had admirers without end," and that Pip "saw her often at Richmond." Estella remains incorrigibly rude and proud in her conduct toward Pip.

The scene then shifts to a meeting of Pip, Estella, and Miss Havisham at Satis House. Pip detects early in the meeting that "Estella was set to wreak Miss Havisham's revenge on men, and that she was not to be given to me until she had gratified it for a term." The revenge that is referenced here is Miss Havisham's having been abandoned by her fiancé on their scheduled wedding day. On the occasion of the visit narrated in this chapter, Miss Havisham and Estella exchange rude words, with Estella accusing Miss Havisham of having twisted her personality to be proud. By the next morning the relationship has returned to normal.

But an even worse development remains for Pip to discover. Drummle has become a member of The Finches of the Grove, the club of which Pip and Herbert are members. When it comes time for Drummle to "toast a lady," the information emerges that Drummle is engaged to marry Estella. Pip's entreaties with Estella to change her mind fall on deaf ears.

This is a chapter devoted to twisted relationships—between Miss Havisham and the child she raised and between Estella and Drummle. Almost everything that unfolds has the quality of an exposé of family secrets. Great storytellers like Shakespeare and Dickens do not need an education in psychology in order to "get it right" in their portrayal of psychology. Estella emerges as a pathetic figure who has given up on life in a "who-cares?" marriage to an unworthy man.

Commentary

This is obviously a major chapter in the love story of Pip and Estella. It is a story of heartache at its most intense. A whole new context is provided as we learn about Miss Havisham's manipulation of Estella as an agent of revenge against men. In a single chapter, Estella moves in our estimation from being just an agent of villainy against Pip to being a victim of abuse from adults herself.

For Reflection or Discussion

How does the chapter advance the characterization of Miss Havisham? Of Estella?

CHAPTER 39

Pip's Benefactor Revealed

Plot Summary

At the end of chapter 37 Pip had foreshadowed the event that occurs in this chapter by calling it "the turning point of my life." At age twenty-three, Pip is seated alone in his apartment (with Herbert Pocket away on business) during a stormy night. A "roughly" dressed man, having the look of "a voyager by sea," knocks at the door and is allowed entry. As the details gradually unfold, it emerges that the man is named Abel Magwitch. He is none other than the convict whom Pip helped at the very beginning of the story. He has lived abroad "in the new world," become prosperous with livestock, and sent the money he earned to make a gentleman of Pip. Pip is repelled by the man.

The fallout from the appearance of Magwitch is huge. Pip is completely disillusioned by the new information, inasmuch as he had assumed all along that Miss Havisham was his benefactor. The visitor asks Pip to find lodging for him, and the apartment is the obvious place. But Magwitch is a convict who had been banished from England for life; if he is captured, he will be hanged. Pip is now harboring a fugitive from justice and lives in moment-by-moment terror.

Commentary

This is one of the memorable chapters not only of this novel but in English literature. We can profitably begin by taking a wide-angle view of the story as structured according to the framework that literary critics call the well-made plot. The exposition of the story occupies the first seven chapters and is devoted to situating Pip in his childhood situation. The inciting moment is the first visit to Miss Havisham's house. The rising action consists of Pip's quest to rise socially and be a gentleman; this has been the main story line from the time of his first visit to Miss Havisham to the moment of the convict's appearance in his apartment. The arrival of Magwitch and the disclosures he shares with Pip constitute the turning point of the plot—the point that changes the direction of the action toward its final resolution. The ensuing phase is called further complication, and in this story it takes the form of Pip's forging a new life and identity now that he has lost his great expectations.

As we move through chapter 39, we quickly see that the material is structured as a back-and-forth movement between Magwitch's divulging a piece of information and Pip's interior thoughts in response to the information that Magwitch has just revealed. By this strategy Dickens does a mas-

One of Dickens's greatest gifts as a storyteller is his ability to use description to evoke atmosphere. The opening paragraphs of this chapter give us a memorable instance of the "dark and stormy night" motif. Of course, setting in a story functions as a suitable "container" of the action, so in this case the storm outside corresponds to the "storm" that occurs in Pip's apartment as the convict keeps talking.

This is not an ordinary suspense story in which we finally learn "who done it." It is not merely that we learn who has been financing Pip's lifestyle. The added punch here is that the anonymous benefactor is *the most unexpected* candidate that we could ever imagine. This is *the least likely motif,* just as in Jesus's parable of the good Samaritan help is offered by the least likely passerby.

terful job of taking us inside Pip's consciousness as he absorbs a terrible shock to his psyche. The overall structure is an ever-expanding revelation of horrors for Pip.

A number of archetypes and storytelling conventions converge to make this the powerful chapter that it is. One is the disclosure of a secret, as when Joseph reveals his identity to his brothers in Egypt. Because the question of the identity of Pip's anonymous benefactor has been kept alive in our awareness throughout the story, this disclosure of the secret falls into such genres as the mystery story, the detective story, and the story of suspense. A related narrative convention that storytellers love is the surprise motif, and this is a prime example of the convention.

But of course there is a deeper level of meaning than these time-honored plot devices. This entire novel revolves around the motif announced in the title—Pip's great expectations. In this chapter Pip's great expectations are systematically taken away from him. Additionally, he is forced to confront the false premises on which he has built his life. Although we do not yet know the details, Pip is about to reenact a familiar Christian pattern of facing the worst about oneself and one's situation as a prerequisite to growth of character.

For Reflection or Discussion

What aspects of Dickens's storytelling technique in this chapter strike you as most noteworthy and effective? What most absorbs your interest? How do you assess Pip's character on the basis of the shifting feelings and attitudes that he shares as the chapter unfolds? A feature of storytelling is that as readers we make provisional predictions about what will

---

The two key paragraphs in the chapter are the fourth and fifth ones from the end, beginning with the statement, "Miss Havisham's intentions towards me, all a mere dream." These paragraphs need to be analyzed in detail as an index to Pip's (a) state of mind in this moment of crisis and (b) moral growth of character as he faces the worst about himself and confesses his failings of the past.

Dickens divided the story into three main sections. Chapter 39 brings part 2 to an end; we read simply, "THIS IS THE END OF THE SECOND STAGE OF PIP'S EXPECTATIONS." The first time we read similar words was at the end of chapter 19, just before the chapter that shifts Pip from the village to London.

happen and then revise those expectations as events unfold; now that Pip's expectations have been taken from him, what do you think he will do?

CHAPTER 40
The Morning After

Plot Summary

The story now takes on a new tone of danger. When Pip goes down the dark staircase the morning after the convict's arrival, he trips over someone lurking on the stairs. The convict eats breakfast ravenously and like an old dog, which reminds Pip of how he ate breakfast in the churchyard at the beginning of the story. Pip decides to attempt to find lodgings for Magwitch in the vicinity under the name of Mr. Provis. While Pip is out, he touches base with Mr. Jaggers, who already knows everything that is transpiring. A change of clothing does little to make the convict look respectable. At the end of the chapter Herbert comes to the apartment and is enlisted as an ally.

Commentary

Pip's life as a man of leisure has had its moments of tension, but the general pace of the story has been relatively relaxed in the middle chapters of the novel. Now a whole new dynamic enters the story and comes to dominate it. The earlier suspense surrounding the identity of Pip's benefactor is now replaced by suspense over whether Pip will be able to keep Magwitch beyond the arm of the law until he can be safely smuggled out of England and back to New South Wales in Australia. The social whirl

Dickens's strategy in this part of the story goes by the name "design for terror"— the invention of details that evoke a sense of fear and danger. To enjoy such a story, we need to be receptive to the narrative thrill of being scared. Dickens gets things off to a good start with a man lurking on the staircase of Pip's apartment.

It is important to the design of this story that we are made to feel the criminality of Magwitch. Numerous details in this chapter bring us into an encounter with the extent to which Magwitch is a criminal. Of course he is more than a criminal, and that is important, too.

of dinners and meeting new acquaintances is now replaced with moment-by-moment fears of discovery and arrest. Pip's life has become a nightmare.

For Reflection or Discussion
How do you respond to the change of pace and shift in subject matter that now suddenly take over the story? What features of Dickens's design for terror strike you as particularly inventive or clever?

CHAPTER 41

The Beginnings of a Plan for Escape

Plot Summary
Herbert and Pip hold a strategy session regarding what to do with the fugitive on their hands. The conversation unfolds exactly as we expect, as based on our own real-life experiences of crisis. Various ideas are floated, and gradually a plan takes shape. In this chapter, it is resolved that the goal is to get Magwitch out of England. Additionally, Pip and Herbert agree that Pip needs to learn more about the fugitive.

Commentary
This is a transition chapter between the onset of fear and the gathering of more information about the fugitive. The function of the chapter is to reinforce the dangerous element that is now a "given" of Pip's situation and to propel us into the next chapter, where Magwitch will provide an account of his life.

One of the books of literary criticism on this novel is titled *A Novel of Friendship*. This should alert us to the importance of friendships in this story. As Pip reflects on how Herbert received him "with open arms" when they met for the strategy session, he observes, "I had never felt before, so blessedly, what it is to have a friend."

For Reflection or Discussion

What is true to life in this strategy session that Pip and Herbert conduct in the throes of fear and a feeling of helplessness?

CHAPTER 42

The Life Story of a Reformed Convict

Plot Summary

In the preceding chapter Pip and Herbert decided that they needed to know the facts of Magwitch's past, and this chapter delivers that history. Growing up in an impoverished milieu, Magwitch had begun a life of petty crime. He crossed the path of a well-educated but criminally inclined man named Compeyson. Magwitch came under the control of Compeyson, and when they were tried for a mutual crime, the well-dressed Compeyson got off with a seven-year sentence and the criminal-looking Magwitch received a fourteen-year sentence. The hostility of Magwitch toward Compeyson explains the scene early in the novel of the two convicts fighting in the mud, with one of them claiming that the other had tried to kill him.

But there are still more plotlines that converge as Magwitch tells his story. Compeyson once teamed up with a fellow partner in crime named Arthur to swindle a rich woman out of her money. Arthur was so haunted by what he had done that he had hallucinations that this woman was his wife, and he actually died of fright. While this story is being told, Herbert writes a note and passes it to

Perhaps Dickens composed this story with an ancient Greek story as a subtext (a template on which an author constructs his or her own story). The story of Oedipus, like the story of Pip, is built on the premise of an orphaned infant who rises to good fortune. Each believes that he knows the details that lie behind his good fortune (in the case of Oedipus becoming king of a realm and marrying the widowed queen of the kingdom), only to find as details are revealed that the premises have been terribly incorrect.

Pip, and we are to trust the accuracy of Herbert's conclusion: "Young Havisham's name was Arthur. Compeyson is the man who professed to be Miss Havisham's lover."

Commentary

The technical term for Dickens's design in this chapter is called flashback, meaning that the content of the chapter takes us back to earlier events in the overall story that the novel tells. And as is often true in flashback situations, it is the readers (more than the characters in the story) who are primarily enlightened by the information that is disclosed. Many more details remain to be uncovered in the network of relationships that Dickens's imagination invents for this novel, but some things are now falling into place.

One of the chief pleasures of a mystery story is that the details that baffle us in the early part of the story suddenly fall into place as we learn the truth. In this chapter, we suddenly understand the behavior and charges of the two convicts fighting in the mud on the marshes.

On the surface, this chapter is devoted to sensational plot material, but it is a mark of great writers that although they do not bypass what the popular readership wants in a story, they do more with that material than lesser writers do. This chapter is filled with recognizable human experiences that we can relate to our own lives and observations: the human propensity toward evil, impoverished childhood as a seedbed for criminality, the corrupting influence of bad company, greed for money and its destructive effects, lying as a means to benefit oneself, the haunting effect of a guilty conscience, the injustice of the judicial system, and thirst for revenge.

For Reflection or Discussion

Why does Dickens devote so much attention in this novel to the world of criminals? How does the chapter fit into the genre of the mystery story or detective story? At this point, does it make any difference that we know the details of Miss Havisham's having been jilted on her wedding day? How does the chapter contribute to our understanding of Magwitch as a key character in the novel?

CHAPTER 43

Pip Returns to "Hometown"

Plot Summary

When Herbert had first proposed that Magwitch must be smuggled out of England at all costs, he also theorized that Pip would need to accompany the criminal. With that as a premise, Pip wishes to make contact with Estella and Miss Havisham before he departs. He goes to Richmond to visit Estella and is surprised to learn that she has returned to Satis House. So Pip makes another return trip to the village of his youth. He checks into the Blue Boar Inn and promptly meets Drummle, who is there to dine with Estella. The entire remainder of the chapter is devoted to the hostile interaction between Drummle and Pip.

Commentary

We are in a phase of action in which Pip's great expectations are slipping away from him. Thus far our minds have focused on Pip's loss of income and lifestyle, and we have forgotten about the love story involving Pip's aspirations to win the love of Estella. This chapter suddenly puts that strand of plot back on the table. Of course it is in the nature of literature that the imagination heightens whatever it touches, so we do not simply witness Pip's

This episode, too, might have a subtext from ancient literature. Epic stories like *The Iliad* are war stories. Epic battles, in turn, resolve themselves into a series of single combats. The exchange of insults is an important part of the rituals of battle in epic stories. Pip and Drummle, too, are engaged in a single combat, and they exchange some delicious insults as they stand before the fireplace.

loss of Estella, but his loss of her to a completely repulsive person.

Yet it is Dickens's habit to treat troubling story material with a comic touch. The scene of Pip and Drummle standing shoulder to shoulder in front of the fireplace of the Blue Boar Inn is one of Dickens's great comic scenes. Leslie Fiedler, in his book *Fiction and the Unconscious*, claims that storytellers intuitively know that when their subject matter is threatening, they need to find ways to enclose the terror within a reassuring framework that has the effect of distancing the terror. If they do not, readers will not experience pleasure in the story and will stop reading.

For Reflection or Discussion

What details in this chapter do you most relish? Why do you think Dickens invents the scene of Pip and Drummle, when he could have brought Pip and Estella together at Satis House without this episode?

Very near the end of the chapter, when Pip watches Drummle ride off on his horse, Pip comes to the conclusion that "the slouching shoulders and ragged hair of this man, whose back was towards me, reminded me of Orlick." The brotherhood of evil keeps expanding in this novel.

CHAPTER 44

Pip Confronts Miss Havisham and Estella

Plot Summary

Pip proceeds from the inn to Satis House, where he finds Estella knitting and Miss Havisham looking on. The first item on Pip's agenda is to settle a score with Miss Havisham. He accuses her of leading him on during the long process of his mistakenly assuming that Miss Havisham was his benefactor.

Secondly, since the Pocket family has been obnoxiously in pursuit of Miss Havisham's wealth, Pip wants to clear the names of Matthew and Herbert Pocket, who remained friends of Pip even after Pip superseded them in Miss Havisham's supposed favor. He also requests that Miss Havisham make a secret donation to settle Herbert in his business, thereby completing what Pip had begun two years earlier.

Then Pip turns to Estella. He berates her for choosing Drummle as husband; Estella offers as explanation that "I am tired of the life I have led." In a particularly moving speech (seven paragraphs from the end of the chapter) Pip professes that he will always love Estella, ending with the outburst, "O God bless you, God forgive you!" Ever afterwards, Pip remembers that as he uttered those words and kissed Estella's hand, Estella "looked at me merely with incredulous wonder," whereas Miss Havisham, "her hand still covering her heart, seemed all resolved into a ghastly stare of pity and remorse."

The chapter ends with a surprise and brief scene of terror. As Pip returns to his apartment late at night, the night porter hands him a note in Wemmick's handwriting with the words, "Don't go home."

Commentary

We are naturally very interested to find out what transpires at presumably the final meeting between Pip and the two most important women in his life. The starting premise is that Pip feels betrayed by both women, and this underlies his accusatory approach to them in this scene. Both women are defensive of their actions and on the

One of the unifying motifs in the characterization of Pip is his position as an abused person. In fact, most of the adults who were leading forces during his growing-up years in the village abused him. In this chapter Pip confronts two women who have tormented him since the age of approximately ten.

The encounter with Estella falls into the category of "tear jerker." The final speech to Estella is intensely moving, and then when Pip leaves the house, we read that "the light of the day seemed of a darker colour than when I went in. For a while, I hid myself among some lanes and by-paths, and then struck off to walk all the way to London [a distance of 26 miles]."

surface concede no feeling of wrongdoing. On a first reading, we naturally assume that this is the culmination of the characterization of these two characters, but that turns out to be incorrect. The two women appear in a bad light in this chapter but will make a remarkable recovery before the story ends.

For Reflection or Discussion

Pip paid this visit with goals in mind; what do you infer those goals were? In what ways did he succeed, and in what ways did he fail? How do you assess the story of Pip's romantic devotion to an unworthy object of that devotion?

CHAPTER 45

Magwitch Changes Location

Plot Summary

Melodrama exists for the sake of exciting external action. To read it in keeping with its literary conventions, we need to give ourselves to the excitement of the plot. In this phase of *Great Expectations*, that excitement consists of danger and the accompanying emotion of fear.

Upon reading Wemmick's note "Don't go home," Pip turns from his apartment and rents a room for the night. He rises early and pays a visit to Wemmick at his house (the "Castle"). Pip joins Wemmick and Wemmick's father ("the Aged") for breakfast and learns that Compeyson is present in London. He learns further that Magwitch has been secretly moved to the home of Clara Barley, Herbert's fiancée. The home is located on the bank of the Thames River. The chapter ends with Pip sitting before Wemmick's fire, catching up on sleep.

Commentary

For several chapters in this phase of the novel, Dickens draws upon a genre known as melodrama. The emphasis is on external action, and in this case the action deals with the danger of the situation, the intrigue by which Pip hopes to smuggle Magwitch out of the country, and the suspense over whether all the planning will succeed in saving the life of Magwitch. This is a conflict between heightened good and evil, another feature of melodrama.

For Reflection or Discussion

The opening account of Pip's dismal night in a rented room is a recognizable experience for any reader; what have been your own versions of Pip's sleepless night in a spooky place? How does Dickens introduce reassuring domestic touches to offset the terror of the convict's situation?

CHAPTER 46

Further Plans for the Convict's Escape

Plot Summary

Pip visits the house where Clara Barley lives with her father ("old Gruffandgrim"), who lives overhead in a frequently drunken state. Herbert is present and confirms the accuracy of what Wemmick has told him. As further plans emerge, it is decided that Pip should make a habit of rowing on the river in the vicinity of the house under the guise of pursuing rowing as a sport. Although nothing sinister happens, Pip has the uneasy feeling that someone is watching him. Magwitch, alias Provis, adopts yet another name, Mr. Campbell.

We cannot remind ourselves too often that *Great Expectations* is, along with many other things, a love story. Sometimes the reminders are subtle. Despite the urgency of the situation Dickens takes time to paint an idealized picture of Clara's worthiness as Herbert's beloved. Then, near the end of the chapter, seemingly out of nowhere, we read, "And then I thought of Estella, and of our parting, and went home very sadly."

Commentary

The story is still controlled by the conventions of melodrama. It has become a suspense story on a grand scale.

For Reflection or Discussion

For you, what are the pleasures of melodrama and the suspense story? Why do you think the human race enjoys being scared when it chooses literary works to read? How does Dickens's skill in creating characters manifest itself in this chapter?

CHAPTER 47

Still More Terror

Plot Summary

The chapter begins with Pip's tallying up the losses that have engulfed him: his loss of income resulting in debts, his impression that Estella has married Drummle, and his anxiety that Magwitch will be discovered. Pip's assessment is that "it was an unhappy life that I lived," with "one dominant anxiety" that never left him. Still, no new terrors emerge until Pip decides to attend a theatrical performance in which Mr. Wopsle is an actor. After the performance, Wopsle informs Pip that he had seen the second convict who was captured on the marshes seated behind Pip in the theater—in other words, Compeyson. Obviously Pip is being shadowed. He decides to share the information with Wemmick by way of a letter.

Commentary

The amount of space that Dickens lavishes on the melodrama of danger surrounding Magwitch might seem unusual or even a betrayal of the serious issues that the novel has "put on the table," but in fact this is a rather common strategy in the annals of storytelling. In Shakespeare's play *Hamlet*, a melodramatic fencing match runs away with the play in its latter stages. In Dostoyevsky's novel *The Brothers Karamazov*, the courtroom drama of Dmitri's trial for murder is the dominant focus for a hundred pages. Mark Twain's *Huckleberry Finn* ends with a long section of melodramatic farce surrounding a fabricated escape for the runaway slave Jim.

We can also ponder a paradox about the mystery story genre. Stories of suspense like this section of *Great Expectations* gain mastery over readers by setting into play two contradictory impulses. On the one hand, the essence of plot is conflict and tension, without which a story does not engage our interest. Thus the story of Pip's increasing danger is at one level what we want. But we also have within us an instinctive impulse to escape from danger and threat, so we try to put an end to it. The clash between these two impulses is what we experience for several chapters in the latter part of *Great Expectations*.

For Reflection or Discussion

How does the struggle between our narrative taste for conflict and tension and our innate desire to be relieved of danger and threat work itself out in your experience of this part of *Great Expectations*? What sense do you make of the typical feature (as noted above) of serious literary masterpieces resorting to melodrama in the latter stages of the story? What is there about the rhythm of narrative that might account for it? How do you personally respond to it?

Yet another literary genre that becomes operative in this part of the plot is literary tragedy. Tragedy depicts a great fall of someone who had been in a position of heightened power and prosperity. As the tragedy unfolds, the tragic hero undergoes "grave spiritual or physical suffering" (says Oscar Mandel in his book *A Definition of Tragedy*). Further, the tragic hero is progressively divested of all that constituted his prosperity, and he becomes an increasingly isolated figure within his world. Obviously all of this fits the situation of Pip.

CHAPTER 48

Pip Learns Who Estella's Mother Is

Plot Summary

As Pip strolls down the sidewalk in central London, he suddenly feels Mr. Jaggers's hand on him. Shortly thereafter Pip finds himself seated at dinner with Mr. Jaggers and Wemmick. Mr. Jaggers produces a note from Miss Havisham requesting that Pip pay her a visit "on a little matter of business you mentioned to her," namely, making a financial donation to Herbert Pocket's business venture. The conversation then turns to the painful subject of Estella having married Drummle.

But these preliminaries are only the warm-up to the real business of the chapter. Pip's attention is arrested by "a certain action of the fingers" of Jaggers's housekeeper. When Pip scrutinizes her further, he "felt absolutely certain that this woman was Estella's mother." As Wemmick and Pip walk away from Jaggers's house, Wemmick fills in the details. The housekeeper had murdered a woman out of jealousy, but Jaggers defended her so cleverly in court that she was acquitted. Shortly thereafter the woman entered the service of Jaggers. The final detail that is established is that the woman had a daughter, implied to be Estella.

Commentary

The comment of a literary scholar rings true repeatedly in the second half of *Great Expectations*: Dickens's later novels have the character of detective stories. Some of the mysteries in *Great Expectations* are posed at the outset, such as the

All of the chapters where the action takes place in London are filled with specific place names. In this chapter we read about Cheapside, Little Britain, and Gerrard Street. Anyone familiar with the area around St. Paul's Cathedral knows exactly where these places are. The result is that *Great Expectations* is at one level a city novel. Additionally, the love of specific places throughout the entire novel easily lifts it into the genre of regional writing. Then if we realize that Dickens has set this story in the places he knew and loved best, we can see a strong autobiographical element in the story.

identity of Pip's benefactor. But others are sprung on us as revelations are made. Probably few readers had been led to wonder up to this point in the story about the parentage of Estella, but now that we know who her mother is, we naturally wonder who her father is. We are told that the housekeeper "had been married very young . . . to a tramping man." Who might the tramping man be?

A second thing to note about this new development is that once again the story plunges into the workings of the criminal world. We relive the cruelty of the murder that Jaggers's housekeeper committed. We also see clearly that Jaggers partly bases his legal career on the perversion of justice.

For Reflection or Discussion

Why do you think Dickens devotes so much attention in this novel to the world of crime and criminals? What is the effect, for you, of his having done so?

CHAPTER 49

Another Visit to Miss Havisham

Plot Summary

Pip journeys to "Hometown" in response to Miss Havisham's note requesting his presence to complete the business transaction regarding Herbert. Miss Havisham is even more frail than in the past, and "there was an air of utter loneliness upon her." Pip requests nine hundred pounds for Herbert, to which Miss Havisham assents. But the personal angle turns out to be Miss Havisham's more pressing concern on this occasion. She hands Pip a paper with her name on it, and then asks Pip to write "I forgive her" if he can ever bring himself to do so. Pip immediately responds, "O Miss Havisham, I can do it now."

Miss Havisham breaks down emotionally. She divulges that it was only at the recent meeting of Pip and Estella at Satis House that she saw what she had done in molding Estella to be her own agent of revenge against men. Smitten with remorse, she also tells Pip, "If you knew all my story you would have some compassion for me and a better understanding of me." When Pip questions her about Estella's origin, she claims not to know who Estella's parents are, having received Estella as an orphan at the age of two or three for adoption through the mediation of Jaggers.

As Pip leaves Satis House, he turns a backward look and thinks he sees again what had proved to be only a phantom when he visited Miss Havisham as a boy: "I fancied that I saw Miss Havisham hanging to the beam." Pip returns to the house, and as he does, Miss Havisham's dress catches on fire. Pip attacks the fire, saves Miss Havisham's life, and finds that his own hands are terribly burned. The chapter ends with one of the truly touching scenes in the novel: "I leaned over her and touched her lips with mine, just as they said, . . . Take the pencil and write under my name, I forgive her."

Commentary

From start to finish, the moral vision of *Great Expectations* is Christian. We can ascertain the moral vision of a literary work by listing what it offers to us as virtuous behavior and what it por-

It is obvious that one of Dickens's greatest strengths as a writer was his descriptive ability, which in turn makes the evocation of atmosphere a leading feature in his stories. The description at the beginning of this chapter of the village (Rochester in real life) is a triumph of atmosphere.

We would be hard-pressed to find a more notable example in fictional writing of the experience of forgiveness than what we find in this chapter. While forgiveness is not exclusive to the Christian faith, we also need to say that it is more central to Christianity than to other religious and moral systems.

trays as vice—its scheme of virtues and vices. In *Great Expectations* the moral pattern is partly established by negative example—by showing us what *not* to do. This chapter devoted to the experience of forgiveness and grace (unmerited favor) is a high point of the moral thrust of the story, and we should call it what it is—a strongly Christian episode in the book.

Another way to view this is to note that Pip is not simply the protagonist of the story; he is also what in literary terms is called the hero of the story. In the first third of the story, we sympathize with Pip because he is a victim, but being a victim is not a heroic action. In the middle of the story, Pip is selfish, complacent, and snobbish—certainly vices making Pip an immoral person, though he never becomes a truly evil person. In the last third of the story, Pip becomes a moral hero, so we should be on the alert for Dickens's systematic elevation of Pip as a moral hero.

Two key ingredients in that heroism have been established by this point in the story. One is Pip's extravagant forgiveness of Miss Havisham and his self-sacrifice in endangering his own life to save her from the fire. Secondly, throughout the "London section" of the story there has been a background chorus of short "asides" in which Pip acknowledges that his shame regarding his humble origins and his snobbishness toward Joe are wrong. We might say that he confesses his wrongdoing but lacks the moral strength to turn from that wrongdoing (repentance). Pip is heroic in having the courage and self-awareness to face the worst about himself.

In the middle of the chapter we find a key paragraph in which Pip analyzes the twisted life that Miss Havisham has brought upon herself and expresses his compassion for her situation. The sentiments that Pip expresses here are thoroughly Christian. A small signal that we are intended to interpret them in a Christian way is the statement that what has happened in Miss Havisham's life is what always happens when people "reverse the appointed order of their Maker."

For Reflection or Discussion

How does your attitude toward Miss Havisham change in this chapter? What growth in Pip's character occurs? How does the moral vision of the book become more established in this chapter?

CHAPTERS 50 AND 51

Pip Learns Who Estella's Father Is

Plot Summary

After numerous long chapters, we suddenly get a short chapter with chapter 50. It packs a big punch, however. Pip returns to London as a recuperating burn patient, and Herbert attends to his needs. The conversation naturally turns to the current state of the convict that they currently harbor. Herbert had spent two hours sitting with "Provis" the night before, and he had told Herbert a good deal about "a dark wild part" of his past. Provis tells a story of having fathered a daughter. The details surrounding the mother of the child make it clear that she is both the housekeeper of Jaggers and mother of Estella. The mother had threatened to murder the child, but the details surrounding her actions were murky at the time.

Nonetheless, fearing that it might be true, Magwitch went into hiding, fearing that he might be asked to give evidence against the mother. In turn, Compeyson had used the situation to blackmail Magwitch. As we end the chapter, it is clear that the girl was not murdered but transferred to Miss Havisham for raising. In short, the benefactor in Pip's life is also the father of the woman he has long loved.

Chapter 51 is devoted to the same story material as chapter 50. The scene shifts to Jaggers's law office, and Pip in effect accuses Jaggers of wrongdoing in not disclosing the mystery of Estella's parentage to him and Magwitch. Jaggers is completely defensive and argues that no good and much harm would have come from divulging the secret.

Commentary

The tangled web of relationships that the novel presents is of course part of the detective story aspect of the story. We can enjoy it as a self-rewarding literary genre. But it is also natural to search for deeper meanings. The only way for *Great Expectations* to make complete sense is to see that the love story aspect is not peripheral to Dickens's design but important to it. Pip's infatuation with Estella is established as a mainspring of action early in the book. The reconciliation of the two, with the implication of a wedding around the corner, will end the novel. Once we grant the importance of the romantic love motif, the emphasis on unraveling the mystery of Estella's parentage makes sense.

Secondly, one of Dickens's "signature" skills is to introduce a multitude of plotlines into his novels and then make them converge in the late stages of the story. We can admire the skill of the master plan as the plotlines converge.

For Reflection or Discussion

How do the developments in the characterization of Magwitch affect your response to him? How does the mystery of Estella's parentage fit into the story as a whole?

Unraveling the mystery of the parentage of an orphaned child is not only perennially interesting to readers of literature; it is also important in real life. The most famous literary treatment of the motif is the mythical Greek story of Oedipus Rex ("Oedipus the King"). As Oedipus pieces together the facts of his parentage, he learns that he unknowingly murdered his father and married his mother. Dickens surely invented his story with the Greek myth as a template, but the case can be made that he gives us a comic (optimistic) version of it, as we learn the heartwarming details that the girl of Pip's dreams is the daughter of the man who lavished generosity on him.

Pip's Narrow Escape on the Marshes

Plot Summary

These two chapters, like the previous two, form a single action. The first piece of narrative business is that Herbert's partnership in the Clarriker business, which Pip secretly helped establish, has flourished to the point that a branch will open in the East, with Herbert in charge of it. Secondly, plans are formulated for proceeding in the attempt to get Magwitch onto an outgoing steamer. With these motifs established, the excitement begins.

Upon returning to his apartment, Pip receives a note telling him to show up on the marshes on the outskirts of "Hometown." Pip makes the journey. He goes to the marshes on a rainy night, enters the sluice house (boathouse), and is immediately pounced on by the villainous Orlick. Orlick is drunk and completely vengeful, accusing Pip of having "come betwixt me and a young woman I liked" (Biddy) and of having been "always in Old Orlick's way since ever you was a child." He also confesses to having been the person who attacked Mrs. Gargery and of having been the lurker on the stairs of Pip's apartment. He confirms that "Old Orlick knowed you was a smuggling your Uncle Provis away." A fight ensues, and Pip yells out with all his might. He hears "responsive shouts," and the door opens to reveal the least likely person imaginable—"the face of Trabb's boy!" Pip has been rescued, and the thing that instigated the entire rescue is that Pip had dropped the note summoning him to the marshes

We should not overlook a very key statement that Pip makes in the opening paragraph of chapter 52. He says in regard to his arranging for Herbert's financial security in his business that "it was the only good thing I had done . . . since I was apprised my great expectations." That assessment is not entirely true, since Pip has brought much good into many lives and has himself experienced growth of character. Yet the statement heightens our awareness of how much money Pip has squandered during his indulgent years in London.

in his room, where Pip's friends Herbert and Startop had found it.

Commentary

The principle of interspersed melodrama reasserts itself in the exciting events on the marshes. The specific genre that Dickens taps into is the adventure story—the story of unexpected and sensational external action. To enjoy these two chapters, we need to cultivate the child's stance of being captivated by frightening events and characters. The genre of the mystery story also continues to explain what is happening, as we now know conclusively who maimed Pip's sister with a blunt instrument to the head. But the excitement in the sluice house is not the only melodramatic ingredient. At the end of chapter 53, as Pip lies recovering in his room, we learn that plans for smuggling Magwitch out of England by boat are moving toward the execution phase.

For Reflection or Discussion

According to literary critic Northrop Frye, literature as a whole is the context within which we read a given work of literature, with the result that as we read we are continuously reminded of similar motifs, archetypes, and conventions in other works that we have read. With this as a premise, what rescue stories in your literary experience (or real-life experience) correspond to Pip's rescue on the marshes? Where have you encountered a villain like Orlick in your literary sojourns or in real life? What "dark and stormy nights" can you summon from your memory to compare to the adventure on the marshes?

The archetype that is reenacted in the adventure on the marshes is the rescue. For there to be a rescue, a person needs to be placed in a helpless situation that threatens him or her. With the situation seemingly hopeless, an outside agent enters and does for the person in danger what he or she is helpless to do. In this episode Dickens gives us a memorable addition to the world's repertoire of rescue stories.

CHAPTER 54

Magwitch Is Captured

Plot Summary

The long-anticipated attempt to smuggle Magwitch out of England finally begins. In a real-life touch, Pip experiences "the relief of being at last engaged in the execution" of a dangerous venture. The boat ride down the Thames River has so many place names that the chapter becomes a piece of regional writing. The suspense is drawn out at length as we are given a moment-by-moment rehearsal of what transpires. At the end of all the strain, Magwitch is captured when Compeyson shows up on the steamer to identify Magwitch as a fugitive from justice. Both convicts go overboard, and only Magwitch returns.

Commentary

The first requirement is that we give ourselves to the excitement and suspense of this adventure story. The point in drawing out the action at such length and in as much detail as Dickens gives us is to heighten the tension and prolong the suspense. Then we need to come to terms with the tragic shape of the action: we were hoping for a happy ending to the ordeal, and our hopes are dashed.

As we know from movies and television dramas, storytellers absolutely love chase scenes. Dickens belongs to the circle of writers who believe that a chase scene late in a story is a perfect way to maintain a reader's interest. So he invented a prolonged chase. To make it even better, he situated the chase on a river. Of course a chase can end with either an escape or capture.

Amidst all the melodrama of this chapter, Pip's moral growth continues. The overall pattern is Pip's loyalty to Magwitch, as seen in his putting himself in danger to help Magwitch escape. It is Pip who remains at the side of Magwitch as the ship takes him to prison. The key statement is this one: "For now, my repugnance to him had all melted away, and in the hunted wounded shackled creature who held my hand in his, I only saw a man who had meant to be my benefactor. . . ."

An important aspect of Pip's story is that he loses virtually everything except his life. Four paragraphs from the end of this chapter he highlights how, now that Magwitch has been captured as a guilty convict, his possessions will be appropriated by "the Crown," that is, the government. Pip's great expectations have been totally removed.

For Reflection or Discussion

Obviously Dickens could have invented a story in which Magwitch escapes; why do you think he chose the opposite path? What are the effects of his having chosen that path?

CHAPTER 55

Developments in Herbert's and Wemmick's Lives

Plot Summary

With Magwitch in prison as a convicted man, Pip and Jaggers come to the conclusion (reluctantly on Jaggers's part) that any hope of salvaging Magwitch's money for Pip has been dashed. A conversation between Pip and Herbert yields the information that (a) Herbert will head up a foreign branch of his company and that (b) he and Clara want Pip to live with them as a clerk in the company. Pip requests two or three months to think about the offer, in-as-much as he has "a vague something lingering in my thoughts" that needs resolution. (We will learn later what those thoughts are.)

With Herbert in effect having moved out of Pip's life as a close-at-hand friend, the rest of the chapter relates developments in Pip's relationship to Wemmick. When Pip meets Wemmick at the door of his apartment, Wemmick expresses the same regret that Jaggers did earlier in the chapter: regret that Magwitch's money has slipped through Pip's fingers (Jaggers's way of saying it) when there would have been ways to secure it for Pip. Wem-

Pip's moral growth during the late stages of this novel is seen partly in the revolution of values that he undergoes. In particular, his worship of money and affluent lifestyle increasingly seem unworthy to Pip. A key moment in this moral growth occurs after Wemmick's comment that "what I look at, is the sacrifice of so much portable property" and Pip replies, "What *I* think of, Wemmick, is the poor owner of the property."

mick is devastated by "the sacrifice of so much portable property. Dear me!" With this regret having been duly registered, the rest of the chapter is devoted to Wemmick's wedding. Dickens chooses to treat it in a comic manner. Wemmick asks Pip to take a walk with him, and the walk is punctuated with such observations as the following: "Here's a church!" "Here's a couple of gloves!" "Here's Miss Skiffins! Let's have a wedding," and "Here's a ring!"

Commentary

This chapter puts two main interpretative concerns before us. We first need to note that Pip's divestiture (the taking away of what he has possessed) continues at a rapid pace. The conversations with Jaggers and Wemmick make it clear that Pip has been left financially destitute. He will need to build his life anew "from scratch." In addition, Herbert's getting married and moving away removes a friend from Pip's life.

Secondly, we can scarcely avoid noticing that a pattern has emerged of young people in Pip's circle pairing off and getting married. Equally, we can scarcely avoid wondering who might be the next to get married.

For Reflection or Discussion

What details in the chapter contribute to the motif of Pip's losing the things that have constituted his life for the past several years?

CHAPTER 56

The Sentencing of Magwitch

Plot Summary

This chapter is devoted to reaching closure on Pip's dealings with his benefactor. That closure takes the form of Pip's attendance at the sentencing of the convict. Dickens takes a final swipe at the judicial system of his day by making the death sentence of Magwitch one of "two-and-thirty men and women put before the Judge to receive that sentence together." Pip is the constant attendant on Magwitch in his final days. Magwitch is so ill that the days are actually a death watch. At the very end, Pip confides that Magwitch has a living daughter who "is a lady and very beautiful. And I love her!" Thereupon Magwitch breathes his last.

Commentary

Two things absorb most of our attention in this chapter. One is the pathos of Magwitch's situation. He is physically ill and exhausted after his watery struggle with Compeyson. He is in prison. He is on death row. He is singled out by the judge as being especially evil.

The second unifying thread is the loyalty of Pip to Magwitch and the moral growth that this represents in Pip. The chapter ends with conspicuous attention to Jesus's parable of the Pharisee and publican. Pip's parting shot is the prayer, "O Lord, be merciful to him, a sinner!" This should not be misinterpreted, as it often is. By praying for God's mercy to be extended to Magwitch, Pip is not placing himself in the position of the self-righteous Pharisee in Jesus's parable. The prayer is

This chapter is filled with gestures of mutual tenderness between Magwitch and Pip. One index to this is the numerous times that Dickens describes the touching of hands between the two men.

"And I love her!" Pip tells Magwitch regarding his daughter Estella. We need to pick up on the clues that Dickens keeps putting before us that he intends to bring Pip and Estella together by the end of the novel.

an appropriate sentiment for a criminal who has just died.

For Reflection or Discussion

What is the satiric thread in the chapter, directed against the judicial system portrayed in the novel? What elements of pathos pervade the chapter? How are we led to see clearly that Pip has moved from the status of a moral nonentity (his life as a gentleman) to a moral hero?

CHAPTER 57

Pip's Death and Rebirth

Plot Summary

Pip reaches the lowest point of his life in this chapter. He is arrested for debt. He has no income. He is suffering from a fever that leaves him delirious. In his extremity, every face that he imagines is the face of Joe. At one point he opens his eyes and determines that it *is* Joe. Joe has come to London to care for Pip. Pip asks about Miss Havisham and is informed that she has died. Another piece of news is that Estella inherited most of Miss Havisham's money, but Miss Havisham did leave "a cool four thousand to Mr. Matthew Pocket," on the strength of Pip's having put in a good word for him.

After extended care, Joe concludes that Pip can look after himself, so he returns to the village. He leaves a letter on the breakfast table with a receipt enclosed that shows that he has paid the debt for which Pip had been arrested. As Pip recovers more fully, he resolves to return to the village and ask Biddy to marry him.

Commentary

The archetype known as the death and rebirth motif has been called "the archetype of archetypes," in tribute to its prevalence in literature and the profundity of the principle that it embodies. Except for stories of literal death and rebirth, this archetype refers to a metaphoric death—a low point that represents a kind of death in a person's life. The first half of this chapter narrates such a situation in Pip's life. His incapacitating illness, accompanied by loss of reason, highlights the motif. "I was like a child in his hands," Pip says of Joe; he *is*, in fact, like a child, a fact reinforced a few lines later when Joe "wrapped me up, took me in his arms," and carried him down to a coach for a ride in the country.

In a novel where friendship is a leading theme, this chapter may be the most memorable entry in the field. Joe's loyalty and generosity are part of the equation, but so is Pip's gratitude. The friendship is reciprocal.

We have no way of knowing it yet, but the last three chapters of the novel (starting here) will be governed by a literary convention known as poetic justice, which consists of virtuous characters rewarded and evil characters punished. In this chapter we read about Pumblechook's house having been broken into and Orlick's being in the county jail for the offense. Pip's noble behavior toward Magwitch is rewarded when Joe looks after him and he recovers his health.

For Reflection or Discussion

How does the chapter reinforce the pattern of Joe's being a moral compass in the novel? What growth can we find in Pip? If the action adheres to the

Throughout the second half of the story there has been an undercurrent of short statements by Pip—"asides" as in a play—in which he accuses himself. In effect Pip is a moral commentator on his failings. In this chapter, we read that the stronger Pip becomes, the less easy Joe feels around him, and that "I soon began to understand that the cause of it was in me, and that the fault of it was all mine." Similarly, when Joe offers the opinion that the two of them had been "ever the best of friends," Pip "was ashamed to answer him."

Joe's exemplary moral behavior is inclusively rather than exclusively Christian behavior, meaning that a person does not need to be a Christian to be generous and compassionate. Nonetheless, an explicitly Christian note is sounded when Pip whispers to himself, "O God, bless him! O God, bless this gentle, Christian man!"

death-rebirth archetype, what things constitute Pip's metaphoric death, and what are the aspects of his rebirth? The most provocative statement in the chapter is Pip's statement to Joe, "I feel thankful that I have been ill, Joe." What do you make of Pip's sentiment?

CHAPTER 58

Pip's Return to the Village

Plot Summary

The London phase of Pip's life is over, and this emotion-laden chapter narrates his return to "Hometown." Much has changed. The Blue Boar Inn puts Pip in "a very indifferent chamber" now that he is no longer wealthy. There are bills posted on Satis House announcing an upcoming auction. Uncle Pumblechook, who had fawned on Pip when he had great expectations, now says to him, "Young man, I am sorry to see you brought low. But what else could be expected!" By the time Pumblechook has poisoned the minds of people on the sidewalk, they look at Pip "with very unfavourable glances."

Hints have been laid that Pip hopes to marry Biddy. He is shocked (and so are we) to discover that he has arrived on the very day on which Joe and Biddy are getting married. This may be the biggest surprise in a novel that is full of them. Pip summons the good will to congratulate them. More than that, he lavishly asks them to forgive him for his ungenerous behavior toward them. The encounter becomes a good-bye scene when Pip asks to have a look at his "old little room" before "we say good-bye."

At numerous times in this guide we have seen that *Great Expectations* overflows with archetypes. The rehearsal of how the very people who catered to Pip when he was wealthy and are now condescending to him once he's lost his great expectations belongs to an archetype of life and literature that we call "fair-weather friends."

Two further paragraphs telescope the action forward and fill in Pip's subsequent life. Pip joined Herbert and Clara in running the Eastern Branch of the Clarriker Firm in which Herbert has a partnership. Pip rises to third in the firm, and the company is said to have "a good name" and to have done "very well."

Commentary

Dickens saves his best descriptive paragraph in the whole book for the account of Pip's progress toward Joe's house. The paragraph begins, "The June weather was delicious." To render the moment even more poignant, Dickens makes Pip a latter-day prodigal son returning home after a journey into a far country: "I felt like one who was toiling home barefoot from distant travel, and whose wanderings had lasted many years."

As Pip expresses his remorse to Joe and Biddy for his bad behavior toward them and promises to repay the money with which Joe paid off his debts, he becomes the ideal penitent. He expresses the hope that if Joe and Biddy have a little boy, he will "grow up a much better man than I did."

The drama of forgiveness that immediately follows this confession could have been handled without introducing Christian overtones into it, but Dickens adds a Christian coloring. Joe says, "God knows as I forgive you." And Biddy adds, "Amen! And God knows I do!"

The concluding paragraph in which Pip summarizes the good fortunes of his business is brimming with latent meanings. First, although this novel is often read as a simple repudiation of the Victorian worship of success and wealth (especially living off the labors of someone else), that is

At the beginning of the next-to-last paragraph, Pip tells us, "I sold all I had." This is a hugely evocative allusion to Jesus's command to a rich young ruler who was so tied to money that he could not obey: "One thing you still lack. Sell all that you have and distribute to the poor" (Luke 18:22).

a misreading. This novel endorses a modified success ethic. Pip does not return to his native village and emulate Joe; he has become far too sophisticated to be satisfied with that. Herbert and Pip's business "did very well," the omnipresent motto of the success ethic. But it is only a *modified* success ethic, not a gross one: the company was never "a great House," nor did it make "mints of money," nor was it "in a grand way of business." A small detail whose significance we should not overlook is that "we . . . worked for our profits," in contrast to Pip's living off someone else's money in the middle phase of the book.

For Reflection or Discussion

This is one of the most important chapters in the book; for you, what stands out most notably? In the scheme of the well-made plot, all that has happened since the night Magwitch showed up in Pip's apartment has been "further complication." We can summarize it in the formula "Pip's quest to establish a new identity now that he has lost his great expectations." What are the ingredients of the new identity that Pip has established? What are the Christian experiences that Dickens places before us in this chapter?

Pip Attains His Romantic Quest

Plot Summary

If *Great Expectations* were not a love story, it would have ended with chapter 58. Chapter 59 is devoted solely to bringing Pip and Estella together, and the fact that Dickens ends his story this way shows the importance he attached to the love interest in this novel. The actual writing is beautiful and evocative and showcases Dickens's skill with description.

Pip returns to the village of his upbringing after an eleven-year absence (which means, incidentally, that he is approximately thirty-four years old). Pip's visit begins with his being reunited with Joe and Biddy in their home. Joe and Biddy have two small children. Biddy claims that Pip "must marry." She also informs Pip that Drummle has died, making Estella a single woman.

The scene then shifts to the remains of the garden adjacent to the place where Miss Havisham's property (now vanished from the scene) had once stood. Estella enters the scene, and she and Pip talk. The drift of the conversation is that (a) Estella has been transformed through suffering into a worthy person and (b) Pip lays claim to her with the final assurance that "I saw no shadow of another parting from her."

It has been obvious throughout this novel that the domestic aspect of life is important to Dickens, as it was to his Victorian culture. Many scenes have been set in homes and around tables. It is true that many of the family relations portrayed in the novel are dysfunctional, but their effect shows the value of a harmonious family by negative example. The domestic scene in the Gargery kitchen that opens this chapter is a fitting climax to one of the unifying motifs in the story.

Commentary

From start to finish, this chapter is slanted around the marriage motif, in keeping with our final understanding that Pip and Estella will

One of the surprises that the novel springs on us is a gradual (or sudden) awareness that although Pip and Estella are far from heroic much of the time (and Estella not until the very end), they *are* heroic. They face the worst about themselves and reform their lives. Irish poet William Butler Yeats said famously, "Why should we honor those who die on the field of battle? A man may show as reckless a courage in entering into the abyss of himself." The humble Joe is virtuous by birthright and therefore grows the least; perhaps Estella is the greatest hero of the story as the one who undergoes the greatest transformation of character.

marry. First, the scene set in the Gargery home is an archetypal domestic scene. Sitting on the stool on which Pip once sat is Joe and Biddy's little boy Pip, "looking at the fire." Pip eats dinner with the family. After dinner Biddy and Pip speak "as [Biddy's] little girl lay sleeping in her lap." Biddy "looked down at her child, and put its little hand to her lips."

After that, we get the equivalent of thirty-foot-high billboards along an interstate announcing "Marriage around the Corner." Here is a sampling: "Biddy said gently, 'You must marry.'" After kissing her little girl's hand, Biddy "put the good matronly hand with which she had touched it into mine," and Pip thinks to himself that "there was something in the action and in the light pressure of Biddy's wedding ring, that had a very pretty eloquence in it." Pip beholds "a solitary figure" in the ruined garden, and it is Estella. Estella is so changed and tender that Pip felt "what I had never felt before," namely, "the friendly touch of the once insensible hand." Pip and Estella "sat down on a bench." Pip tells Estella, "You have always held your place in *my* heart." Pip and Estella leave the garden hand in hand (which as one literary critic correctly observes, is not a prelude to parting). Etc., etc.

Additionally, the atmosphere evoked is completely conventional for what we call "a love scene." The setting is a garden at twilight. The couple is seated on a bench. The following specimen of description follows such a familiar path that if the key words were left blank, we could fill them in with the right words: "A cold silvery mist had veiled the afternoon, and the moon was not yet up to scatter it. But, the stars were shining beyond the mist, and the moon was coming, and the evening was not dark."

Most decisively of all, though, we have the final conversation between Pip and Estella. Estella raises the possibility of parting, but Pip rejects it with the firm statement that "I saw no shadow of another parting from her." Estella recalls the earlier farewell scene when Pip had said, "God bless you, God forgive you," and asks Pip to say it now. Most important of all is Estella's comment, "Now, when suffering has been stronger than all other teaching, . . . I have been bent and broken, but—I hope—into a better shape." As with a camera click, *Great Expectations* takes its place in the mainstream of Western literature, where the tragic motif of wisdom through suffering has been a major subject of imaginative literature, from the Old Testament book of Job through Greek tragedy through Shakespeare's *King Lear* to Dickens's *Great Expectations* and beyond.

To ensure that we attach sufficient weight to the conclusion, in the final paragraph of the book Dickens introduces an evocative allusion to the final lines of Milton's *Paradise Lost*. The last two lines of *Paradise Lost* narrate how Adam and Eve "hand in hand, with wand'ring steps and slow, / Through Eden took their solitary way" in the twilight of the day of the fall. Similarly, Pip tells how he "took her hand in mine, and we went out of the ruined place [a garden] as . . . the evening mists were rising."

For Reflection or Discussion

The first thing to do is trace in detail the ways in which Dickens manages the material in such a way as to embody the experience of romantic love

In the manuscript version of the story, the story concludes with Pip and Estella parting. A literary confidant persuaded Dickens to change the ending, and he did. In the very nature of things, it is the published version that constitutes the author's final intention. Dickens himself wrote in a letter that he "should never have permitted the publication of the second ending, had I not been convinced it was superior."

A comment by literary critic Northrop Frye is worth its weight in gold if we apply it to the conclusion of this novel: "E. M. Forster once remarked that if it weren't for wedding bells or funeral bells a novelist would hardly know where to stop: he might have added a third conventional ending, the point of self-knowledge, at which a character finds something out about himself as a result of some crucial experience."

culminating in marriage. Secondly, the transformation of Estella from hardened soul to worthy person needs to be probed. Then we need to take the whole sweep of the story into account and explore what makes this chapter, and preeminently the final paragraphs, a satisfying conclusion to the story as a whole.

The Moral Vision of *Great Expectations*

A word of explanation is in order about the division of duties between this page and the next one. Morality concerns people's relations to other people. Religion touches upon people's relation to God and the spiritual realm.

The moral vision of a work of literature is easy to determine. All we need to do is analyze and then list in two columns the behavior that the work offers for our approval as being virtuous and the actions that it portrays as vices. The moral vision of *Great Expectations* is broadly Christian. Before we explore that, it is useful to make a distinction between "inclusively Christian" ideas and "exclusively Christian" ideas. If we draw two circles, one representing Christianity and the other representing other religious and ethical systems, there is obviously a large overlapping area; this is inclusively Christian material (it includes Christianity as well as other systems). There is also much that is exclusive to the Christian belief system, falling outside the overlapping area.

The moral vision of *Great Expectations* falls mainly into the overlapping, inclusively Christian category. The novel exalts the following virtues and gives us memorable examples of them: love, self-sacrifice, forgiveness, exercise of duty, contentment, humility, generosity, loyalty in friendship, compassion, honesty, industriousness (willingness to work diligently), patience, kindness, and politeness. Assimilating the novel's embodiment of these virtues reinforces a Christian's moral sense and makes a person wish to live the moral life.

Of course the story partly elevates those virtues through negative example, commending them to us with examples of characters who do *not* exercise the virtues. This brings us to the other half of the moral equation—the list of vices in the story. *Great Expectations* gives us examples that lead us to view the following vices as reprehensible: selfishness, self-centeredness, rudeness, pride, bullying of others, violent behavior, laziness, mean-spiritedness, greediness, coldheartedness in place of a loving spirit, isolation from others, refusing to grant forgiveness, manipulation of people for one's own advantage, dishonesty, fostering injustice, and victimizing others. *Great Expectations* devotes as much space to portraying these vices as it does to displaying virtuous behavior, but this half of the equation contributes just as much to establishing the moral vision of the story as the portrayal of virtues does.

Literary critic Angus Calder sums up the situation by saying that Dickens "judged his characters by absolute standards of right and wrong which have a very explicit Christian basis."

The Religious Vision of *Great Expectations*

The religious vision of a literary work consists of how the work envisions (if it does at all) God and the spiritual world. Additionally, whereas the moral vision of a work focuses on virtues and vices, the religious vision can be phrased more in terms of *values* that the work regards as important and/or unimportant. *Great Expectations* is a book that requires our very best thinking as we piece together its religious vision. It is possible to understate and overstate the Christian vision of this novel.

We should start by noting what is *not* present. Nowhere do we catch a hint that God is the supreme being in a person's life; in fact, we get no picture of God at all. We hear nothing about the salvation of one's soul, the forgiveness of one's sins in Christ, or the existence of heaven now and in the afterlife. At this level there is an alarming secularism about the book.

Nonetheless, there are many aspects of the story that are either Christian or congruent with a Christian view of life. To begin, the world portrayed in the story is a Christian world. We read about churches and cathedrals, and about people who attend church and pray. The characters sometimes express Christian sentiments, use Christian vocabulary, and echo the Bible. If these seem unimportant, we can profitably contrast the world of this novel to the world we encounter in virtually all movies and television dramas, where we would never catch a hint that anyone ever attends a church service or reads the Bible.

Secondly, the story gives us examples of patterns that are congruent with Christian realities, even if it does not portray them as being specifically Christian. Most important of all is the way in which Pip's life embodies some very important Christian paradoxes. He finds his true self by losing himself (his false identity). He loses the world (defined in terms of material prosperity) but gains his soul (in the sense of becoming a morally good person whom we admire). Pip dies to earthly success and is reborn as someone who lives for the right values.

If we then ask what values the story elevates to supremacy, the picture is again congruent with Christianity, even though the primary value of love of God is absent. One approach is to see the progress that Pip makes in seeing the inadequacy of the values on which he has built his life. He repudiates self-seeking, social prestige, and an affluent lifestyle. He embraces the values of friendship, home, family, marriage, and contentment with a simple state of life. There is much that reinforces a Christian worldview for readers who start with Christian convictions themselves. The story provides a critique of materialism and self-centeredness, and so does the Bible. This story embodies a warning against living by false values and shows how to live by true values; so does the Bible.

Finally, there are the biblical connections that have been noted in the commentary in this guide. They are not extensive, but whenever they surface, they remind us that the author was familiar with the Bible.

Further Resources

While virtually any edition of the novel will provide a good version of the text, two editions contain "critical apparatus" that is sympathetic to Christian readings of the book: the Ignatius Critical Editions version includes interpretive essays in the back of the book, and the introduction to the older Penguin edition (but not the current one) by Angus Calder is outstanding (published by Penguin 1965–1976).

The following books, arranged alphabetically by author, were selected either for their superior value as repositories of literary commentary on *Great Expectations* or as books that illuminate the religious and moral dimensions of the book.

Cotsell, Michael, ed. *Critical Essays on Charles Dickens's "Great Expectations."* Boston: G. K. Hall, 1990.

Epstein, Norrie. *The Friendly Dickens: Being a Good-Natured Guide to the Art and Adventures of the Man Who Invented Scrooge.* New York: Viking, 1998. A collection of materials on all things Dickensian.

Goodheart, Eugene, ed. *Critical Insights: Great Expectations.* Pasadena: Salem, 2010. Specifically the essays "A Second Level of Symbolism in *Great Expectations*" by Elizabeth MacAndrew (pp. 161–176) and "Christian Allusion, Comedic Structure, and the Metaphor of Baptism in *Great Expectations*" by John Cunningham (pp. 177–195).

Hake, Steven R. "The Power of a Life: *Great Expectations* as a Christian Novel." PhD diss., State University of New York at Binghamton, 1990.

Hardy, Barbara. *The Moral Art of Dickens.* New York: Oxford University Press, 1970; also published by Athlone Press in 1970 and subsequently.

Hornback, Bert G. *Great Expectations: A Novel of Friendship.* Boston: G. K. Hall, 1987.

Lettis, Richard and William E. Morris, eds. *Assessing Great Expectations.* San Francisco: Chandler, 1960.

Ryken, Leland. "Dickens' *Great Expectations* and Literature as Recreation." Chap. 7 in *Realms of Gold: The Classics in Christian Perspective.* Wheaton, IL: Harold Shaw, 1991.

Walder, Dennis. *Dickens and Religion.* London: George Allen & Unwin, 1981.

Glossary of Literary Terms Used in This Book

Adventure story. An action-packed story of spectacular events, often (but not always) involving the fantastic.

Allusion. A reference to past history or literature.

Archetype. A plot motif (such as the quest), character type (such as the villain), or image/setting (e.g., darkness) that recurs throughout literature and life.

Character/characterization. The persons and other agents who perform the actions in a story.

Dramatic irony. A situation in which the reader knows something that one or more characters in the work of literature do not know.

Foil. Anything in a story (for example, a character, plotline, or setting) that *sets off* something in the main story by being either a parallel or a contrast.

Genre. Literary type or kind, such as story or poem.

Gothic literature. Literature that exploits terror or horror, and also the mysterious and supernatural. Staples include haunted houses or castles, midnight scenes, dungeons, graveyards, ghosts, and monsters.

Melodrama. A narrative that features sensational external events. The plot conflict is between obvious right and wrong, and characters likewise fall into a pattern of heightened virtue and vice. Other elements are exaggerated emotions, thrilling action, and reliance of coincidence.

Motif. The literary term for pattern (a series of examples of the same thing).

Narrative. Synonymous with story.

Novel. A long story that employs the techniques of realism and avoids elements of fantasy.

Plot. The carefully organized sequence of actions and events that make up a story, arranged as one or more conflicts that reach resolution.

Poetic justice. The rewarding of virtue and punishment of vice.

Realism. Lifelikeness; literary presentation of characters, events, and settings that really happen in our world.

Satire. A work of literature that exposes vice or folly.

Setting. The places where events in a story occur; can be temporal as well as physical.

Theme. An idea about life that is embodied in a work of literature and that can be deduced from it.

Well-made plot. A framework that modern literary criticism devised to show the pattern and unity in a carefully constructed story. The well-made plot unfolds in the following order: exposition (explaining the ingredients that make the story possible); inciting moment or inciting force (the thing that begins the action or plot conflict); rising action; turning point (the point that signals how the plot conflict(s) will eventually be resolved); further complication; climax; denouement (tying up of loose ends).

HAWTHORNE'S
THE SCARLET LETTER

HOMER'S
THE ODYSSEY

MILTON'S
PARADISE LOST

SHAKESPEARE'S
MACBETH

BUNYAN'S
THE PILGRIM'S PROGRESS

Encounter the classics of Western literature with literary expert Leland Ryken and learn to evaluate the text from a Christian worldview.